Anger Management

How to Control Anger, Master Your Emotions, and Eliminate Stress and Anxiety, including Tips on Self-Control, Self-Discipline, NLP, and Emotional Intelligence

Contents

Introduction

Anger. An unpleasant emotion which can lead to equally unpleasant consequences if left unchecked. Generally speaking, anger is an extreme emotional response to something that disturbs us. We feel antagonism and strong irritation because something has gone wrong and there seems to be unkind intent from a perpetrator and a desire to cause us harm. Anger is mostly directed toward those we know – friends, family, coworkers – and usually, the expression of it is vocal. Aggression, the violent element that is sometimes a part of anger is less common, although it does exist. The question is how do we control it?

The problem with anger is that in some instances, for some individuals, it is difficult to control. It can turn into road rage, a boardroom yelling match, or a wrongful death suit directed at a doctor who really wasn't culpable. In fact, the worst thing about moderate anger isn't what it makes us do to others, but the negative influence it can have on the person whose anger goes uncontrolled. How many of us have fired off an email at a perceived insult, only to discover we misunderstood the point or didn't have all the information needed to understand what was going on? That is the anger we need to learn to control, and there are methods and keys in learning to do that.

This guidebook will detail everything that you need to learn regarding how to reign in your anger issues once and for all.

Chapter 1: What is Anger & Where Does It Come From?

Anger is something that is present in everyone. All of us have had moments of "meltdowns" or when we "completely lost it" with friends, family, coworkers, even perfect strangers sometimes. It happens to the best of us. It only becomes a problem when it happens more frequently than it should and when it happens at extreme levels.

Depending on how you handle it, anger can be something which is both good and bad. When used for good, anger can drive you and motivate you to change for the better. For example, when you see an injustice happening, feeling angry about it fuels your desire to make a change for the better. It can lead to groups that rally and come together for a change to be better like the march for women's rights or animal rights. When anger is used for bad, though, it can lead to terrible things like physical abuse, confrontations that escalate into violence and even worst-case scenarios: murder. Many have gone to jail because they murdered someone in the heat of the moment. That is what happens when anger is left unchecked and out of control. Prolonged anger among friends and families can lead to unhappiness, years of not talking to one another, and ruined relationships.

The problem with anger in some people is that they find it hard to let go. Have you ever had moments where you recalled an argument or a confrontation you had, and the mere thought of it just makes your blood boil all over again? That's what anger can do. It makes you hold onto grudges and unable to forgive, let go and move on.

What is Anger Anyway?

It is one of our core emotions as a human being. Humans are indeed unique creatures, capable of feeling several types of emotions, sometimes even a few emotions at once. Happiness, sadness, joy, anger, disgust, fear, bravery, anxiety, despair, all these are just a small example of the range of emotion we are capable of. It is these emotional states which have helped us survive.

Anger, just like our other emotional states, is used to describe the way that we feel and it helps us identify and connect with what is happening around us. When we are feeling unsafe in a situation, for example, we identify that we're feeling scared or insecure. When something makes us happy, we describe it as joy or happiness. Our emotions are sensitive to what is going on in our surroundings.

Anger is an emotion which has been closely linked to the "fight" or "flight" mechanism which is inbuilt in all of us. It is a way that we respond when we perceive something as a threat. Back when our ancestors were still living and hunting for survival, this emotion helped to keep their minds sharp and simulated, ready for any kind of action.

Where Does It Come From?

Physiologically, we can break down our anger-response to hormonal levels. The amygdala area of the brain triggers response to irritating information or frightening situations. Our "fight or flight" response to annoyances is related to the hormones the brain releases, primarily epinephrine (adrenaline) and norepinephrine (noradrenaline). These hormones result in emotional and physical responses to make us alert and energized. We sometimes call the ensuing sensation an "adrenaline rush" which may lead us to shout obscenities at the judge who is about to determine our prison time, or in extreme fear (an emotion closely related to anger physiologically) lift a heavy tree off of our seven-year-old son. This rush of energy is useful in some situations and probably was even more useful when early humans found themselves face-to-face with a raging beast a bit more often than we do today. So, while managing our anger (and its sister – fear) is important, we wouldn't want to completely disarm the system that sometimes goes into overdrive, causing us to overreact.

Physically, anger can cause other symptoms besides the surge of energy we associate with it. Our hearts often pump faster, and our breathing becomes shallower and quicker. Some people break into a sweat as the blood courses more quickly through their bloodstreams, and rising temperature may lead to the red faces we see in cartoon stereotypes of angry people. While anger is a "hot" emotion, however, fear causes the temperature to decrease – one of the few differences between the body's response to anger and fear.

So that is the physical response to anger, but the psychological response is equally important, and it is our thoughts and behavior that we can adapt to manage anger successfully. Just seeing scratches on our pretty blue car isn't enough to cause an angry outburst for most people. We must also associate someone else with the outcome. Even then, most of us do not act on our anger.

We may vocalize our irritation. "Darn it. I am so tired of that Suburban taking up two spots in the front parking lot! I wish Fred would park where the spots are bigger or get a smaller truck!" We may even fantasize about having the vehicle towed or boxing it in with two other cars. If we don't see or suspect a perpetrator, the response may even shift to sorrow or another emotion. When anger is the appropriate emotional response – when we see that we have been injured, identified a perpetrator, and perceived malice in that act of injury – it is not wrong for us to feel anger. A conversation with Fred about his Suburban may clear the air. However, how we channel that anger may be deeply inappropriate.

When it is justifiable – we watch someone steal our phone or we learn that the promotion we worked hard to earn has been given to a newcomer to the business with a family tied to the CEO – anger makes sense, and the trick is mostly to control the anger and channel it into something more productive than a loud or violent response. That productive path may end up helping us get a better job or perhaps a new and better phone.

What Causes Us to Feel Angry?

Although humans have come a long way and evolved since the time of our ancestors, this emotional state still remains (although it too has evolved since then). The emotional bursts of anger that we feel today still have some similar ties to that of the early humans. For example, when our loved ones are in danger or have been wronged, we feel anger at the perceived threat and want to spring into action to defend them.

In moments of anger, we make poor decisions. We lose all sense of rationale, and our emotional intelligence ceases to exist. All we feel is pure rage (in extreme cases), the blood pounding in our veins, and our muscles become tense and angry. Anger is a raw emotion that can lead you to do things you ordinarily would not do. Anger seems to hijack all our common sense and makes it impossible to make good decisions when we are consumed by this emotion. All we end up doing is either hurting ourselves, the people around us, and feel full of regret with how badly the situation was handled.

There could be several factors which cause you to feel angry. Different people would have different emotional triggers that set off this reaction. Some examples of what could cause a person to feel angry include the following:

- You feel angry when you experience an unfair treatment against you or someone else.

- You feel angry when you are powerless to stop something.

- You feel angry when your goal is not accomplished.

- You feel angry when you think you (or someone else) are being treated unfairly or unkindly.

- You feel angry when promises are broken.

- You feel angry when someone has lied to you.

- You feel angry when you have been disappointed or when you feel disappointed in yourself.

- You feel angry when you are ignored or mistreated.

- You feel angry when you think you're being neglected.

- You feel angry when you experience verbal or physical assault.

- You feel angry when you experience other bad drivers on the road.

- You feel angry when you have to work with colleagues who are either difficult or not on the same page as you are and it is affecting your work.

- You feel angry when you do not get your way (perhaps this is something that you're used to).

Many possible scenarios and situations could cause a person to get angry or upset. One of the things that you need to do towards learning how to manage your anger would be to identify the triggers that set you off so you can then learn to recognize them.

How Do I Know If I Have an Anger Problem?

Do you wonder if your anger ranges in a healthy or unhealthy range? Worried you might have an anger problem? There are several indicators which could help you identify if your anger is indeed something you should be concerned about. How many of the following indicators can you identify with?

- It is hard for you to get over your anger. When you feel angry, you let it simmer and boil within you until it explodes and everyone else around you feels your wrath.

- You can hold a grudge for years because of your anger. You know people whom you have not spoken to for a very long time because you still feel anger towards them.

- You find yourself feeling depressed easily and too frequently, not realizing that this could be a result of repressed anger issues. You find yourself having dangerous suicidal thoughts, perhaps even have tendencies of violence.

- You are unable to express your anger appropriately, choosing instead to bottle it up within you. This could be dangerous too because it may lead to other emotional problems.

- Holding onto your anger is preventing you from living a meaningful, happy life. You constantly find yourself feeling disgruntled, irritated, and frustrated more than you are happy and even the smallest of instances could set you off because of it.

- People have often described you as a very angry individual.

- You're verbally, emotionally (sometimes even physically) abusive towards others around you. You find that it spills over not just into your personal life, but professional life as well.

- You have been called abusive.

- You do not openly express your anger, but you find other ways of channeling it. For example, you're cynical and sarcastic towards yourself or others, or you have adopted a pessimistic outlook on life. This is not a good thing because it can lead to great unhappiness not just for you, but the people around you too.

If far too many of these indicators ring true to you, then you could have a potential anger problem. The first thing you would need to do is accept that your anger is a problem. There is no sense in denying it any longer if you want to fix the situation and learn how to manage your anger better. It needs to begin with acceptance on your part. This is something that no one else can do for you.

You don't have to beat yourself up over it, though, if you do indeed find that you have anger issues. Consider this – *you have valid reasons to be angry*. True, the way that you are expressing that anger may be unreasonable and unacceptable, but you are not getting angry for no reason. You may have good reasons to be angry, but do not use those reasons as an excuse for your behavior. Nothing is ever worth emotionally, verbally, or physically hurting the people around you especially your loved ones. Those kinds of scars can take a long time to heal if they ever do heal at all.

Your anger is triggered by something, and now that you know your reasons, it is time to learn how to manage the second part of the process.

Common Myths about Anger

Before we begin learning how to manage anger better, it is important to break through some of the common myths and misconceptions that you may or may not have regarding anger. This will help develop a deeper understanding of what anger is (and what it isn't), and you will be able to use that understanding to better work on your management techniques.

Here are some of the most common myths about anger that need to be dispelled:

> • **Myth – Men are angrier than women.** This is not true as women can be equally as angry as men can. In fact, research has shown that women could get angry just as frequently as men can and both sexes have an equal chance of being just as angry as the other. A man's anger may be more intense than that of a woman, but women can hold onto anger for much longer than a man can.

> • **Myth – Anger is only a problem if you show it.** Anger which is not expressed can be just as much of a problem.

Repressed anger is similar to how a volcano works. It bubbles and boils under the surface until one day when something sets you off, all that repressed anger just comes shooting out with catastrophic consequences. Anger which is not expressed or shown is just as bad as anger which is blatantly displayed.

• **Myth – The older you get, the angrier you become.** This isn't entirely true. In fact, the older you get for some people, the calmer they are because they know what they want. They know that it simply is not worth it to get angry over trivial matters anymore and they have learned from experience that sometimes it is just not worth getting angry at everything that bugs you.

• **Myth – Anger is a bad thing.** Again, not true, as we described earlier in this book how anger can also be used for good and become a motivating factor. Anger can have many different functions and purposes. It is entirely how you use it. Do you use it to drive you, energize you, or inspire you? Or does it do the complete opposite? That is entirely dependent upon how you handle the situation and your anger.

• **Myth – Anger is all about getting revenge.** That would depend on the individual. This is not true for everyone. For some, revenge is not even something that they think about or getting even could be a secondary motive. It is not always all about revenge, sometimes getting angry is just a way of "venting" or letting out the frustration that has built up within you. For some, their anger only lasts a brief moment, and once it is over, they're back to their old selves not even thinking about it anymore.

• **Myth – Only some "types" of people have anger issues.** This isn't true. Anyone can have anger issues no matter where they come from or what their background may be. It does not necessarily mean that only those who come from broken homes, have a bad record, or non-respectable members of the community have tendencies towards anger problems. Anyone can have anger issues, even that policeman directing traffic on the street or the respectable lawyer working in the city. Grandparents, physicians, homemakers, poor people, rich people, children, professors, scientists. Anyone can be capable of anger issues because anger is an emotion that *everyone* experiences.

Is Anger Affecting Your Health?

Yes. When left unchecked, anger could directly and indirectly affect your health. It is causing health problems without you even realizing it. Some examples of how anger is *indirectly* affecting your health include the following:

- It increases your risks of a heart attack because of the constant stress that you feel.

- It also increases your blood pressure and cholesterol levels, making you prone to having health-related problems because of that stress.

- It could cause obesity (stress-eating, ring a bell?)

And how it is *directly* affecting your health includes:

- Anger affects your decision-making process. You can't make rational, appropriate decisions when you're blinded by anger all the time.

- It drives you to physical injuries. For example, you could punch something in anger which ends up hurting you. Or worst, you could punch someone else which causes physical injury to another person. Neither of which is good, of course.

- Anger could drive some towards alcoholic tendencies.

- Anger could lead to road rage.

- If you drive while you're feeling angry, it makes it difficult to concentrate on your driving which increases the risk of car accidents happening.

These are just a few examples of how anger issues can cause detrimental effects to your health, and you may not even have given it much thought until now – which is why it's now more important than ever that you learn how to manage your anger once and for all.

Chapter 2: Types of Anger Issues – The Good, The Bad, and The Ugly

Some people have a shorter fuse than others, which would explain why they get angry much quicker and more frequently. Often when this happens, there is rarely any time to take control of the situation before it gets out of hand. But why do some people have such a shorter fuse than others? Before we get into the good, bad, and ugly side of anger and what it can lead to, let's take a look at some of the potential reasons behind why you find yourself losing your temper more often than you should. It could be attributed to a number of factors:

- **Your temperament** – Remember how we mentioned that all individuals are unique? This is the perfect example to illustrate that point. We are all different, and therefore, our personalities and our temperaments are different. Not all of us are wired the same way. Some act quicker, while others need more time to process their next move. Some jump to action without thinking twice, while others need more time to ponder the consequences. Some people are more outgoing and adventurous, while some are more laid back and introverted. And in this same way, some people just have a shorter fuse than others do. Our differences are what make us unique.

- **Your personality** – What type of personality would you say you have? Are you generally impatient? Impulsive? Confrontational? Dominating? Bossy? Demanding? Judgmental? If you've answered yes to one or more of these personality traits, then it could explain why you tend to have a shorter fuse than others do. Competitive personalities tend to have shorter fuses too because those with this personality type generally insist or demand that things go their way.

- **The examples you had** – Who were your role models growing up? Did you have parents or other family members who quickly got angry? Sometimes the reason for our short fuses is because that is all we can identify with. That was the example that we had growing up. We don't know any other way because this is how we were raised. If one or both of your parents had a tendency to become angry quickly, chances are you're likely to have that same tendency too.

- **High stress levels** – Are you constantly stressed all the time? Excessive stress which just seems to consume you? You can't even remember a moment when you were *not* feeling stressed. Stress could also act as a potential trigger for a short fuse, leading to abrupt outbursts, temper tantrums, and irrational behavior. It is your body's way of reacting to the stress that you already feel.

- **Do you suffer from mood disorders?** – It could be another reason why you find yourself being angry quickly. An undiagnosed personality disorder could be the trigger for your short fuse without even realizing it. Bipolar disorder, depression, and anxiety are all potential triggers because it won't take much to make you angry. If you do suspect you may have any of these mood disorders, it is best that you seek professional help and don't leave it undiagnosed.

- **Are you getting enough sleep?** – A lack of sleep could also act as a potential trigger for a short fuse. Have you ever noticed how things seem much harder or require more effort when you're feeling tired and fatigued from lack of sleep? You feel cranky, irritable, and even the smallest of things seem like a big deal. That is because your body is tired, your nerves are frayed, and a lack of sleep makes you less efficient than what you normally would be. Therefore, it doesn't take much to set your temper off when you're sleep deprived.

• **How do you view the world?** – What's your outlook on life like? Do you see the world as full of possibilities? Do you wake up each morning with optimism? Or do you have a rather cynical, hostile view of the world around you? The glass is always half empty, and there is no silver lining in sight. When things don't work out the way that you expect them to, it sets off your temper, and you lash out at anything or anyone that may be close by.

• **You have poor communication skills** – When you have a hard time making yourself understood or expressing yourself, it can result in frustration. Poor communication skills can lead to a lot of misunderstanding, which could lead to arguments which cause your temper to rise because you feel like your point is not getting across. Poor communication skills are yet another potential trigger for why you may have a shorter fuse than others.

• **Are you always quick to blame?** – Do you jump at the chance to shift the blame towards someone else? Is it always someone or something that is responsible for your misfortune, never yourself? Do you believe that the "bad" things which happen to you are often a result of someone else's mistakes? Feeling like this all the time is a sure-fire way to a shorter fuse because it makes it so easy to be angry at the world and everyone in it when there is always someone else to blame.

The Good

Earlier in Chapter 1, it was briefly touched on how anger – when used the right way – can be a tool which is used for good. Let's start by looking at some of the positive aspects of our physiological anger response.

Scientists have found more than one advantage to a state of anger. It is short-acting and energizing. It can lead to focus, organization, and clear thinking. Individual results may vary, but since anger is a hormonal response to a specific type of emergency, many people will find that words come to them more easily, their physical strength temporarily increases, and they become minutely and clearly focused on the problem at hand. Professionally, well-channeled anger leads us to seek out solutions and communicate with those who can help instigate change.

When anger is good, and on a healthy level, sometimes it does not even look or feel like anger at all. The occasional irritation is the most that you would feel if your anger was within the healthy range. Good anger will not show up as any kind of aggression at all. This is why anger can sometimes be a good thing. When it is aligned with your values, emotional intelligence, integrity, passion, love, and beliefs, it can motivate you to take positive action without having to rely on aggressive, domineering behavior at all. People who experience healthy anger know that violence and arguments are never the answer, so this is never an option for them.

Anger, when used for good, can spur the following actions:

- It leads you to take precise and direct action

- It motivates you to push past your challenges without perceiving them as a threat

- It gives you the courage to take the necessary action

- It helps you focus on a clear goal

- It awakens your internal fire and passion for making a difference

- It helps you stay in control without the need to explode or lose your temper because you know how to manage your emotions

- It helps you take responsibility for your actions because you understand that blaming someone is never going to do anyone any good

- It empowers you to push past your boundaries and rise to challenges

- It can become one of your greatest assets, pushing you to do what needs to be done

When anger is brought out in intimate relationships, it can result in a discussion of problem areas or lead to creative solutions. Anger at young children is often useful in instigating positive change (mostly in the adult). Since angry adults know they are larger than their children and could hurt or frighten them with a loud or physical response, most angry parents are careful to harness their angry feelings — say to the crayon scribbles all over the new wallpaper, and work quickly to find a solution (quite literally) that will help wipe the problem away.

Another helpful aspect of anger is that it doesn't last too long. Remember the comic book hero the Incredible Hulk who would swell into a green monster when he was angry, act out his rage on whatever vehicle, laboratory, or drug lord was in his way, then collapse exhausted and shrink back into his usual modest self?

The rapid transition out of the throws of anger is one reason that even when anger causes bad outcomes, they are usually not truly horrible. Anger just takes too much out of us to be maintained. Long-maintained anger is never as focused as the short-term variety, but it can lead to high stress levels, which have bad effects on our nervous, circulatory, and pulmonary systems.

So When Does it Start to Get Bad and Ugly?

An example of when your anger turns bad or ugly is when you would relate yourself to a sleeping lion. Everything is all right until something sets you off and you fly into a rage. This is when your anger becomes toxic because other people start to find it difficult to be around you. They always have to be on their guard, nervous and anxious, careful about the way they behave and the things they say because they don't want to send you into one of your rage episodes. Anger becomes toxic when it starts to poison almost every aspect of your life. It ruins your relationships. Other people don't feel safe being around you and you find that people often make excuses to avoid you. This is when anger turns from good to bad and ugly.

Ugly anger is the variety we see in the Incredible Hulk (before he collapses). It is often physically harming, aggressive, and violent, yet is still usually directed toward someone the aggressor knows. The worst of anger occurs when it is both violent and directed toward someone who cannot defend himself or herself. Aggressive and violent anger is often domestic, directed toward a partner, child, or elderly relative. It is criminal behavior.

Frequently, extreme anger is linked to other mental processes that are not operating optimally. If an angry parent is also drunk, then he or she may not have the ability to control the angry response as quickly when a child misbehaves. If he or she is angry and also mentally unstable, even due to a biochemical miswiring, such as General Anxiety Disorder or Chronic Depression, it can exacerbate angry impulses. Both alcohol and drugs (prescribed or recreational) can dull judgment and cause us to dismiss the inner voice that suggests it is time to calm down.

If we are angry and hungry, angry and ill, angry and tired, angry and feeling persecuted, angry and misled, angry and cold, angry and anxious, angry and out in the desert sun... any of these combinations can make it harder for us to allow our rational understanding of the situation at hand to take charge and quickly reset our response to something more appropriate for the situation.

Let's Evaluate How Angry You *Really* Are

While everyone gets angry, it is the *severity* of the anger and the way that it is managed that makes the difference between someone who experiences anger on a healthy spectrum and someone who has anger issues. Not everyone experiences anger to the same degree and that is also what makes the difference.

To start determining how angry you really are, you need first to be able to clearly identify and define what anger is. Anger is:

- An emotion which often either precedes or accompanies aggression

- An emotion that describes the way you feel towards your enemies or people you hate

- An emotion that makes you want to fight

- An emotion that makes you feel like you want to seek revenge

- An emotion that makes your blood boil

- An emotion you feel towards something you perceive as a "threat"

- An emotion that sets a negative precedent or tone

- An emotion that you feel brings out the worst in you

- An emotion that brings the aggressive side of your personality to the surface

Next, we need to identify how often you find yourself feeling angry. Start by answering the following questions:

- How often do you find yourself feeling angry? In the past week, for example, how many times did you find yourself feeling angry or irritated?

•What would your answer be in this instance?

    -I didn't feel angry at all

    -Maybe once or twice

    -Three to five times

    -Five times or more

    -I felt angry almost every day, several times a day

Anything that is more than three to five times a week means that you've got anger issues. But that's okay. The point is to be honest with yourself, even if you don't like the answer. Only then can you begin working to fix the problem.

Let's now assess your anger on a scale of one to 10.

- **Number 1** – Nothing really bothers you for long. You're happy, calm, and generally easy going. It takes a lot to set your anger off, and even then, it doesn't last for long.

- **Number 2** – You feel slight irritation and irritability from time to time, but it never lasts for very long. You usually get over it really quickly. Sometimes you do experience it on a higher scale, but it isn't enough to get you all worked up and distract you from what you should be doing.

- **Number 3** – You keep your anger on the inside and still respond negatively to people. Your anger and irritation are still not high enough to affect your decision making, but other people around you can start to tell that you are feeling annoyed.

- **Number 4** – You feel like you want to yell at someone who is in your way or telling someone off because you're feeling angry and irritable. You start to imagine scenarios in your mind where you are telling people off. You begin to contemplate actually acting on those feelings, but your anger is still not strong enough for you to take action just yet.

• **Number 5** – You start to feel angry at every little thing, and you may even feel angry at yourself. You can still control your reactions and your behavior, but it is now very obvious to everyone around you that you're feeling quite angry and irritable.

• **Number 6** – You start to feel like you could really tell someone off by this point and it is becoming harder to conceal your anger. You might bite someone's head off occasionally, but you are still making an effort to try and reign in your anger. It is getting harder though.

• **Number 7** – Anger is starting to affect you physically. Your muscles start to get tense, the vein in your temple starts to throb, and it feels like your blood is starting to boil. It is becoming harder to control your anger as you feel it creeping up to higher levels.

• **Number 8** – Your anger has now reached a point that you feel you want to do something about it. You want to yell at the person who is annoying you. You want to exact revenge on the person who wronged you. You start to feel a strong desire to inflict hurt or pain because you feel so angry. It is becoming harder to maintain a level head.

• **Number 9** – You've started acting on your angry impulses. You're yelling, shouting, telling people off, using verbal cues to let everyone know that you are *not* happy and telling them exactly what you think. Your anger is starting to rule you by this point, and you no longer care that your words may be hurting someone else's feelings.

• **Number 10** – By this point, you are now a danger to yourself and others around you. By this stage, you could resort to physical violence because you are so blinded by anger that you simply do not care anymore. Your anger has completely taken over, and you are no longer acting like yourself.

Where would you rate yourself on this scale in most situations? Where do you think you constantly hover around? This will give you a good indicator of how angry you really are most of the time. An emotionally healthy individual usually does not venture far from numbers 1 to 3. When anger becomes toxic is when you find yourself living in the 8 to 10 range all the time in almost every situation, even when it is not something serious.

Chapter 3: How to Find Control – Bad Anger, Long-Term Anger, and Explosive Temperament

Now that you know what causes anger, where it comes from, the good, the bad, and the ugly, it's time to get on to the important part – how to control that anger. Whether it be bad, long-term, or even the explosive temperament type of anger, the bottom line is that you want your anger kept in check, not just for your sake, but for everyone else around you too.

Anger can take on various forms. Some people feel angry but only for a brief moment and then they no longer dwell on it. Some people can't stop dwelling on anger, and it could take them hours, days, weeks, months, or even years to get over it. If they get over it at all, that is. Then, there are those who – when they do lose their temper – release their anger in what is known as explosive rage episodes.

No matter what form your anger may take, there is one thing that they all have in common – they are bad for your health and emotional state of being. Not only that, but harboring so much anger within you all the time can lead to risky, violent, and dangerous behavior patterns. It could further lead to problems like drug and alcohol abuse. Health-related problems as we have seen include coronary related heart disease. Other health problems which could result from severe anger issues include insomnia, headaches, muscular aches, and even digestive problems. Possibly the worst consequence, however, is the damage that it can do to your relationships, especially with the people who matter the most.

Tips to Start Learning How to Control Bad, Long-Term, and Explosive Anger

A common misconception about anger management is that it simply means you're learning how to *suppress* your anger. Suppressing your anger is not the goal. The goal here is to learn how to *control* that anger and to understand why you are reacting the way that you are. To learn how to respond better without jumping to anger as your first immediate reaction. To be able to walk away from situations which would have normally aggravated you without losing control. *That is the goal* of learning how to control your anger.

We do not want to get rid of anger entirely because remember that anger is part of the normal range of human emotions. To get rid of it entirely would be unnatural, and more importantly, you would lose out on the good benefits that healthy anger can do – which is why you need to learn *control* rather than suppression or elimination. The more you learn to control your anger, to express it in much healthier ways, the better it will be for your health, your happiness, and your relationships.

Start learning how to control your anger by:

> • **Acknowledge your anger** – Denying your anger issues is one of the worst things you could do. More importantly, it will not help you learn to control it. Facing your problems may not be something that you want to do, but living in denial and ignoring it never solved anything either. If you do have anger issues you need to contend with, it is time to acknowledge them so you can actively do something about it. The more you deny your emotions and anger issues, the worst it will be for you when it comes to managing it. In fact, you may find yourself feeling angrier and losing your temper

even more because you feel helpless and unable to control the situation.

- **Exploring the *reason* behind it** – Anger problems will always stem from something: your childhood, a previous traumatic experience, your role models growing up, or your stress levels. All these things add up and could build towards anger problems. To begin learning how to control your anger, you must first explore and connect with the *core reason* of anger. Your first line of response is how you control it. Anger is very often a response that is meant to cover-up other feelings which you may have. What are those feelings? Jealousy? Embarrassment? Hurt? Shame? Insecurity? These are the reasons you need to explore to know what your anger is covering up for you.

- **Changing the way that you think** – Don't expect other people to "accept" your anger because this is who you are and this is part of your personality. That is entirely the wrong approach to use. In fact, that is just you making excuses to justify your behavior without having to do anything to change it. You need to start changing the way that you think and realize that it is *your responsibility* to manage your anger issues. Other people should not have to tolerate or conform to your expectations. A social setting is not just about you; it is about everyone. Each person is equally important. Instead of expecting other people to conform to you, choose instead to *want to change to be better*. Think about how good it will feel to learn how to control your anger, for the people around you not to always be cautious and wary about when you're going to lose your cool next.

- **Practice deliberately slowing it down** – Emotions can get the best of you, especially anger, which is why learning to slow down your thoughts and emotions deliberately can go a long way towards helping you learn how to control your anger. Have you noticed how when you are starting to feel angry, your thoughts begin to race and get muddled up? Your breathing quickens, and suddenly it becomes difficult to keep a clear head, and you react based on your impulses instead? What you need to do now is to practice slowing your thoughts down to make sure that you are in control, not your anger, at every step of the way even when you're on the verge of getting angry. This can be achieved through practice. For example, what you could begin doing is when you next read something, read it slowly and deliberately focus on what you're reading. When you're writing something, focus on each word you're writing instead of going through the motions. This is how you practice being in control, by focusing on each thing that you are doing.

More Strategies that Can Be Used to Control Your Anger

What else can you do to get rid of this short fuse that you have? Changing your temperament is certainly not going to be an easy process, that's for sure. However, learning to control your anger can certainly be done with the help of the following techniques.

•**Learn to walk away** – If this is something you've never done before, now is a good time to start. This is going to require you to work hard to fight all your natural instincts to fight back at the situation or person that is making you angry. It is going to require you to swallow your pride and learn to walk away from a fight. It is time to wake up and realize that no amount of fighting and arguing is ever going to remedy all of a situation, so it is time to take the next best approach. By choosing to walk away until you've calmed down, instead of staying and fighting, you minimize the risk of having your anger escalate even further to a point you might do something you'll end up regretting. By disengaging yourself from the situation and allowing yourself some breathing space to calm your nerves, you're taking the mature approach in handling any person or situation. Responding in anger is never the solution, and you'll have a much better chance of a positive outcome if you choose this approach. Choose to walk away.

• **Distract yourself** – Anger can cause a lot of damage because it is such a disruptive emotion. All common sense just seems to go out the window in the heat of the moment. In Chapter 1, we talked about learning how to recognize the triggers that tend to set you off and cause your anger to escalate and this is why – because you need to distract yourself. When you recognize your triggers, it makes it easier to put a stop to it, to deflect your attention elsewhere until you've forgotten about what it was that was threatening your temper. You need to distance yourself from the triggers for as long as it takes until you are properly distracted enough that you forgot what it was you were about to feel angry about.

• **Let go of the need to always be right** – And to always have the last word. Why? Because it simply is not worth it. Anger occurs within a social context, and often arguments can go on forever if two people refuse to back down. Somebody always needs to have the last word, and this time it is *not going to be you.* By continuing to indulge in this behavior, you're not helping yourself or your anger issues. You are just making things much worse. Let go of the desire and the need to always be right. Yes, you're going to have to swallow your pride again and fight all your natural instincts to do so, but it will be worth it. It will get easier over time, and you'll feel a sense of satisfaction because, deep down, you know that it is the right thing to do. To put an end to anger or prevent it from escalating, somebody needs to make a move in the right direction. Why not you?

• **Use visualization** – Each time that you feel your anger is threatening to break through the surface, you need to stop immediately, close your eyes and start to visualize. It may sound silly, but it works. Visualization is an effective way to learn to relax, and it will help remind you of the goal that you need to accomplish. The goal here, in this case, would be learning how to control your anger. Picture peaceful scenes which will help you maintain a state of relaxed calm each time that you need it. This can be achieved with practice, and you will need to be able to vividly picture peaceful settings as though they were right in front of you. If the beach is a place you love that has been able to calm you down in the past, picture that. If it is a beautiful garden, picture that. Picture anything that infuses you with a sense of calm and even happiness if possible. This is a great distraction technique too. Being able to visualize and see your end goal will remind you of why you are doing what you are doing and help you to stay on course.

•**Exercising both mind and body** – This is the best outlet to channel all that anger and frustration that you are carrying around inside you. Exercising both your mind and body is a way of redirecting those feelings of anger towards a healthier release mechanism. Instead of taking your anger out on the people around you, channel it into your workouts. If you're doing kickboxing, for example, channel it into every punch and kick you make during the routine. If you're running, channel that energy out through every step that you take as your feet pound the pavement. Exercising both your mind and body simultaneously through yoga is another fantastic approach to take. Yoga is one of the best exercises you could encompass into your daily life because no other exercise medium combines both physical and mental training in one go. Yoga has been used for years as a way to strengthen both the mind and the body and is not just about getting rid of the energy that wears you down, but also building and strengthening yourself mentally, so it is better able to maintain control and keep your anger at bay.

• **Do something that makes you happy** – This is one of the oldest tricks in the book, yet it continues to remain one of the most effective. People who struggle with anger issues have a lot of misery and unhappiness inside them. How can you learn to control your anger if you're still harboring all that negativity inside you? There's nothing better at getting rid of all those unhappy, miserable feelings than very simply doing something that makes you happy. Indulge in a passion or a hobby. Throw yourself into an activity that you love. As much as anger and negativity can affect how you feel, it works the same way when you actively do something which makes you happy. With a happier state of mind, it makes it easier to think with a clearer head. You don't get as worked up so easily anymore, and it becomes much easier to learn how to control your anger issues. So, get out there and start doing all the things that you love again.

• **Breathe mindfully** – Mindful breathing is a useful exercise to have on hand because when faced with anger, you tend to lose control of your emotions. Whenever you're under stress and feeling angry, do you notice how your breathing becomes shallow and more tagged? By learning a few effective breathing techniques, you can dramatically control your response to a situation or a person. Mindful breathing is an exercise that takes practice, and it is something which is simple and easy to do right. You can practice this in your home or anywhere that you can find a quiet spot, and you should aim to practice this exercise often until you can see a difference in the way that you react to situations. Practice mindful breathing by sitting comfortably in a relaxed position, close your eyes, and focus on each breath that you take. Breathe deeply in and out, slow and steady, focusing on each inhale and exhale. Focus on the air that is flowing in and out of your body. Breathe in deeply through your nose and exhale slowly through your mouth. As you breathe in, count to five, pause, relax, and exhale while counting to five again. This repetitive exercise will help you relax, remain calm, and learn to be in control of your breathing patterns.

Whenever you feel your anger rising, straight away change your focus to your breathing and begin mindfully breathing until you have successfully calmed yourself down again.

• **Keep a journal** – Journaling may not be for everyone, but when it comes to controlling your anger issues, it can be very therapeutic. More so than you may realize. One of the problems when it comes to anger is that you're so overwhelmed with all sorts of emotion (anger, frustration, irritation) that it all comes out all at once, especially when you have been keeping it bottled up for so long. Many people tend to strike or lash out in anger because they don't have proper channels or outlets to release that anger unto. This is where a journal comes in handy. Why would a journal help? Because a journal is something that is only for your eyes and it provides you with a safe and private place where you can express every feeling and emotion you have without the fear of being ridiculed or judged. More importantly, it is possibly *the safest* outlet for you to release your feelings of anger without hurting anyone or yourself in the process. Expressing your emotions in a journal will not cause problems or conflict with anyone because it is only for your eyes. Your journal is also a place where you can record the things that happened to you, and pour out all of your feelings of anger until you feel better.

A Few Other Good Tips to Keep in Mind

Because anger can be a difficult and challenging emotion to learn how to master and control, a few additional strategies come in handy. If you're finding it a challenge to change your thought patterns and the way that you react in anger, try the following strategies as reminders or affirmations that you can do this:

• I will not allow my anger to get the best of me. I am in control today and every day.

• I am capable of learning how to control my anger.

- I am in control of my thoughts and my reactions. I always have a choice to respond the right way.

- Anger is only temporary. Therefore, I will not let it get the best of me.

- I acknowledge that I am experiencing feelings of anger right now and I will do my best to calm myself down.

- I will not let my anger escalate out of control again. This is a challenge I can overcome.

- Every day I am getting better at controlling my anger. Every day I am stronger.

- I have more control over my emotions and reactions than I realize. I can do anything I set my mind to, and I choose to be in control.

- I want to get rid of anger issues so anger will not be a driving factor in my life anymore.

Chapter 4: Reexamining Angry Thoughts – How to Handle Long-Term Anger that Doesn't Go Away

Overcoming anger issues is a long journey. That is because there are so many aspects involved and so many challenges to overcome. Learning how to manage your anger is not just about learning how to handle your emotions and how to respond appropriately when you feel your anger rising. Anger management is also about *choosing what kind of person you want to be.* Do you want to become someone who is angry, resentful, bitter, and alone most of the time? Or do you want to become someone who is changing for the better? Someone with self-control, emotional intelligence, and the discipline needed to take control and manage your anger once and for all?

Let's start by reexamining your angry thoughts and why you have found it so hard to overcome long-term anger prior to this. Ask yourself the following questions:

- Have I identified the source of my anger?

- If I am currently feeling angry right now, why is that? What provoked this emotion? How long have I been feeling angry?

- Why am I finding it so difficult to let go of this anger?

Although you do have a right to experience anger (everyone does), you need to consider *why you find it hard to let go* of that anger? Is holding onto this anger for so long something that is justifiable? More importantly, is it worth wasting your precious time and energy being this angry all the time?

Overcoming long-term anger is something that only you can do. Nobody else can do it for you. If you're expecting someone else to apologize for being the cause of your anger, you will be waiting forever, especially if they have already forgotten about it and moved on. Now, it is up to you to do the same. Allow yourself time to be angry and express that anger appropriately, but learn to move on quickly.

To help you with this process, you can start by listing five ways that your life will be much better if you were to forget and let go of your long-term anger. That's a good place to start.

Other tools which you could use to help you reexamine your thoughts and learn to manage long-term anger include self-discipline, emotional intelligence, and neuro-linguistic programming, better known as NLP.

How Self-Discipline Helps Handle Long-Term Anger

The good news is this is *exactly* what you can do. To handle the long-term anger that you've been battling with for so long, not only do you have to reexamine your thoughts, but you need to *increase your self-discipline* too. Why do you need self-discipline to help you manage your anger? Because it is the answer you've been searching for. The key to *why* you haven't been able to manage your anger all this time.

Inside you, there is a power that you didn't know you had. The power to make the positive changes that you long to see in your life.

To tap into that power, you need to have self-discipline. It helps you stay on track towards achieving your goals, towards reaching your full potential. In this case, the goal here is how to manage and handle the long-term anger within you that you've been struggling to conquer all this time.

Self-discipline and self-control are two traits which are not that far apart. The reason that they can help you learn how to manage your anger is that these two qualities help you with the ability to control your impulses, emotions, and behaviors. This ability is also sometimes referred to as willpower, and it is a quality that has helped drive many people towards success. This will now be your key to successfully learning how to manage and control your long-term anger. Everyone can learn how to build a healthy self-discipline habit. It is simply up to you whether you choose to do it or not. Once you do, you will be amazed at what a tremendous impact it will have on your life and your attempts at learning how to manage your anger. You will see what difference it can make.

Self-discipline is such an important skill set to possess. Among the benefits that this trait brings includes:

- Helping you stick to the decisions that you make, to keep on going when the going gets tough.

- It gives you the extra push and the drive that you need to smash through obstacles.

- It helps you with self-control, making it less likely that you're going to give in to your desires and temptations. In this case, self-control helps you manage your anger.

- It helps stop you from reacting impulsively based on your emotions, which are what you need if you hope to control your anger.

- It helps you to stay focused on what you're doing.

Anger is often a self-control issue. You are unable to control your impulses and your responses because you don't have the willpower and the discipline (yet) to get a handle on your anger before it rises to the surface and erupts. Learning how to control your anger is something that has to start *inside* of you, and it needs to start with self-control and self-discipline. You have the power within you to tell yourself:

- I *WILL NOT* lose my temper

- I *WILL NOT* explode

- I *WILL NOT* hold onto my anger any longer

- I *WILL NOT* let my anger rob me of any more joy

This is not stopping your anger, but rather, it is you *declaring what you are going to do.* That is self-control and self-discipline. It helps you take charge and take the control away from your anger.

To begin building habits that will improve your self-control and self-discipline, use the following strategies:

- **Get rid of excuses NOW** – There is no more room for excuses if you're going to learn how to manage your long-term anger. When you're reexamining your thoughts, ask yourself how often you make excuses to justify your behavior? Too often? Then it needs to stop right now. It is time to kick those excuses out the door and into the bin where they belong. Self-discipline leaves no room for excuses – only action.

- **Make a list & write it down** – Make a list of all the changes that you want to see happen so that it is clear as day right in front of you. Making a list is one of the most underestimated tools around, and it cannot be stressed enough just how useful it can be. As human beings, we are very visual creatures. Something becomes more believable when we can see it in front of our eyes. So write down your goals and what you hope to achieve in learning how to manage your anger, and each time you feel your willpower waning, whip out the list and take a good, hard look at it again.

• **Be persistent** – This is such an important quality to have as you work on improving your self-control and self-discipline. It can be so easy to give up when things get tough, but persistence is living proof that you have it within you to achieve anything that you set your mind to. When you persist through one weakness and overcome it, you feel a sense of accomplishment, which will be one of the most rewarding feelings you will ever experience. Persistence makes you appreciate every accomplishment and makes every victory taste just a little bit sweeter. It shows you that you are capable of anything that you set your mind to. Each time you push through a challenge with persistence, you emerge stronger, victorious, and better than when you first started. This is what you need on your side as you begin working on improving your self-discipline.

• **Know what you want** – You can't find the motivation and the drive that you need if you don't know what you want. In this case, you need to tell yourself that you *want* to learn how to manage your long-term anger issues. Ask yourself why you want to achieve this so badly? What is the purpose of you doing all of this? You must be able to specifically answer each question with conviction and belief. That is how you build up the self-discipline that you need to learn how to manage your anger – by remembering *why* you're doing this and *what* you want to accomplish at the end of this journey.

• **Prep yourself mentally** – Your mind is your most powerful tool, and this is going to be the key to increasing your self-discipline levels. Prepare yourself mentally by using positive affirmations, listening to motivational podcasts, reading inspirational books, whatever it takes to prepare you with a positive mindset that will help you stick to this course of action and see it through.

If you're not disciplined enough to put in the work and the effort, you're never going to accomplish the results that you want and learn to master your long-term anger.

How to Manage Long-Term Anger with Emotional Intelligence

Emotional intelligence can be a wonderful tool in helping you manage your long-term anger and reexamine your angry thoughts because of the five components that emotional intelligence is made of. The five core principles include having self-awareness, self-regulation, empathy, social skills, and motivation. These five principles are essential to learning how to manage your anger and reexamine your thoughts because it forces you to stop and reflect, to see beyond your anger.

Self-awareness allows you to view your emotions from an objective standpoint, to take a step back and reflect on why you're feeling such a strong emotion, which in this case is anger. It allows you to make the connection between your heart and your head so that your reactions are not ruled entirely by your emotions (heart). This is how you begin reexamining your angry thoughts – by using self-awareness to reflect upon why you feel this way and use the thinking part to assess what needs to be done about it. Self-regulation, on the other hand, helps you *control* your responses, to stop you from reacting impulsively from a place of anger. It works together with self-awareness and by being fully aware of your anger, its triggers and its causes, it puts you in a much better position to determine what you need to do and what the best approach would be by regulating your behavior when you're angry.

Another emotional intelligence trait which will help you reexamine your angry thoughts is empathy. This is the ability to put yourself in the other person's shoes to understand where they are coming from. It is not just about your anger and the way that you are feeling; it is also about them. If you are feeling angry, what about them? If they are feeling that way, then *why?* And is it for the same reasons you are? Using empathy and social skills in tandem will help you better work through the problems that are causing your anger to rise because, for all you know, the other person you're having a conversation with could be on the same page as you are. It is through empathy and social skills that you will come to an understanding. Combine that with the motivation and determination to *want* to learn how to control your anger, and you will have a much better chance of amicably resolving the argument, without anyone having to have their feelings hurt.

How to Manage Long-Term Anger with Neuro-Linguistic Programming (NLP)

NLP is a concept that focuses on the language that your mind speaks. It is about understanding what your brain is trying to tell you. Without this understanding, it would be challenging to connect yourself to your thoughts, which would then make it more difficult for you to reexamine your angry thoughts. You need NLP to help you connect with your mind and understand your thoughts in a way you have never been able to before. This is how you will learn to manage your long-term anger.

In moments of anger where your emotions rule the situation, NLP is how you will take control again. This concept can help you make a deeper connection between why you are holding onto your anger for so long and open you up to new ideas and possibilities to be more in tune with what's happening internally. To manage your long-term anger issues, you must be able to identify your current limitations and break through them.

NLP's primary concept is about learning how to tap into the unconscious part of your mind and become more adept at managing your emotions. It helps you learn how to manage the situation according to the circumstances you're in, which will help you empathize on a deeper level and maybe see things from a whole new perspective. Suddenly, what was making you so angry may not seem so important anymore, but you won't realize that until your mind and your emotions can make a steady, strong connection to one another.

There are several concepts in NLP which can help you manage your long-term anger issues, one of which is called the Perceptual Positions technique. This NLP strategy teaches you to see things from the other person's perspective which also helps to build up your empathy skills and social skills in the process. With greater levels of empathy, you will develop a better understanding of the people around you which will give you something else to focus on other than your anger. This, in turn, will allow you to see that there are more important things than anger to think about, which will hopefully make it easier for you to let go of any anger you've been holding onto all this time.

And when it comes to reexamining your thoughts, NLP's Content Reframing technique is an excellent strategy whenever you feel that all you can focus on is the negative. Reexamining your thoughts means you need to reframe the way that you think about them. Instead of just seeing them as thoughts which are fueling your anger, *reframe* them into something that empowers you by changing the meaning that you've been associating that thought with all this time. Instead of seeing it as a thought that is causing you anger, see it as a learning lesson instead, an experience which taught you something new. By reframing the way that you think about your angry thoughts, you will be able to see things from an entirely different perspective, and with new focus points to think about, you'll realize that maybe what was making you so angry was not really that big of a deal after all.

Expressing Your Anger in Healthy Ways with Communication Skills

Good communication skills require two things: that you be an active, good listener and you see things from the other person's point of view (like empathy). Empathy is a skill that we all lack when we are angry, just like it was highlighted in the emotional intelligence section above – which is why something else you can learn to do to manage your long-term anger is to learn how to communicate effectively.

Expressing your anger effectively through communication skills is not so much about what you say but *how* you say it. The louder you speak, the less you will make yourself heard. Think about it, would you listen to someone who was yelling at you? Shouting right in front of your face? Definitely not – you would shut down immediately and completely block out what the person is trying to say.

The thing is, when you're busy yelling your head off in anger, you don't realize that the message you are trying to convey gets lost in translation. If you want to be heard, you need to work on your volume and the speed at which you speak. The angrier you are, the faster and louder you tend to speak. However, these two aspects are what you need to start working on if you want to avoid irritating the person you're talking to and having the discussion escalated into a full-blown argument. You start speaking a lot faster when you're angry too. Do you notice that? It is as if you can't wait to get your anger out quick enough. Stop, pause, and pace yourself if you want to make yourself heard.

Other strategies you could use to still communicate effectively while managing your anger at the same time include the following:

- **Keeping it short and concise** – As angry as you are, you need to make an effort to keep the conversation short and concise. It makes it easier for the person on the other end of the conversation to follow your thought process and listen to what it is you're trying to say. This helps to prevent long, drawn-out arguments too which only end up with more hurtful words being exchanged on both ends. You may be angry, but remember that lashing out at the other person is not going to do anybody any favors. Avoid long and unnecessarily elaborate explanations to keep the conversation effective and assertive. This way, you get your point across and say what it is you want to say while still sticking to the facts and key points. This is how you effectively handle a conversation in anger.

• **Highlight your empathy** – Imagine that you're in a heated argument. You're angry, and you're trying to let the other person know *why* you're upset. When that person responds with, "I hear what you're saying, and I can see where you're coming from," doesn't that make you feel so much better? Expressing empathy is how you can effectively handle an angry conversation and keep it from escalating any further. Long-term anger is often a result of feelings of dissatisfaction, feeling like you still have not said your piece, and there's more you would like to get off your chest. You feel like the other person still doesn't "get it". This could contribute to you being unable to let go of your anger and holding onto it for a long time. The next time you're in a heated argument, try expressing your empathy and see what difference it can make to the situation.

• **Manage your tone of voice** – To effectively communicate in an angry argument, you will need to exercise a lot of self-control on your part. This will allow you to remain assertive yet calm enough not to start yelling and be blinded by anger. Self-control is going to come into play with the way that you manage your tone of voice to make sure that your volume is not escalating with every sentence that you speak. A challenging exercise to master in the beginning but it can be done with patience and practice.

• **Under no circumstance should you be forceful** – Do not force the person you're in conversation with to go along with your way of thinking. That is not being an effective communicator; that's on the verge of bullying. You'll be crossing that fine line and venturing into angry aggression. You can still get your point across while communicating effectively during a heated conversation by still choosing to be respectful towards the people you're speaking to.

Acknowledge and respect that you have no control over what other people think or the way they behave, and the best thing you could do for yourself and everyone else is to be firm with your own decision, but still remain calm and respectful even though you may be feeling angry. That is how you effectively manage your long-term anger and keep it from becoming an explosive rage episode.

Chapter 5: Methods for Dealing with Anger – Relaxation Techniques, Letting Go, and Forgiveness

If only staying calm and collected was as easy as losing our tempers! The world would certainly be a much better place, wouldn't it? Getting angry can certainly make your blood boil and your blood pressure rise, which is why it is important to learn how to relax and calm your nerves before things spiral out of control. High blood pressure is a condition that is for life, and once that happens, you're looking at a lifetime of medication just trying to keep it under control. Is your anger worth risking your health like that? No, it most certainly is not.

Learning to Relax and Keep Your Cool – Effective Relaxation Techniques to Help You Calm Down

Relaxation techniques are going to be the best thing for you when it comes to dealing with your anger. This helps prevent you from getting out of control and doing something that you will regret later on. If this has happened far too often than you'd like to admit, perhaps it is time to start adopting these relaxation techniques to help you calm down.

Relaxation Technique #1 – Exercise

One of the best relaxation techniques that can do wonders to improve your health overall is exercise. And it doesn't cost you a thing (unless you join a gym or classes of course). Whether you realize it or not, your lifestyle habits play a big part in the current state of your health. If you're dealing with anger issues, it is likely you've already experienced firsthand some of the effects that anger can do to you. Internal factors such as high levels of stress daily, emotional issues and problems, feeling unhappy and worked up are also factors that can contribute and eventually lead to high blood pressure over a prolonged period. All of this is related to anger, which is why it can cause a lot of the heart-related diseases that we talked about in the previous chapters.

This is why, as part of your relaxation process, one technique you should turn to is exercise. Exercise is good for you. Exercise helps not only to elevate your mood but as your body gets fitter and stronger, your energy levels will increase, and you'll find you're able to accomplish so much more in a day. Exercising also helps to boost your endorphin levels, the hormone which helps you feel good and feel happy. If you're holding onto a lot of anger issues, this is certainly something that you are going to need. Exercising is a channel, an outlet for you to let out any frustration or stress you may have so that it isn't bottled up inside you. Just speak to anyone who works out regularly, and they will be able to attest to how much better they feel after they've done a workout. Exercise is an excellent relaxation technique that can help teach you how to manage your stress and how to release and let go of any current stress you may be carrying around with you. The next time you feel angry and worked up, try doing some exercise. Notice a difference in how you feel?

Relaxation Technique #2 – Yoga

Yoga is another great method of relaxation whenever you're feeling stressed and angry. Why is it so great at helping you relax? Because it focuses on slow, controlled movements. It doesn't put much strain or stress on your body's muscles but instead focuses on building strength through controlled movements. Yoga centers mainly on three main principles to help you achieve a state of calm: meditation, deep breathing techniques, and controlled physical activity.

Meditation teaches you how to breathe deeply and mindfully, drawing more oxygen into your body which helps your blood flow better. It gives you something to focus on other than what is making you angry. Deep breathing teaches your mind and body to relax, opens your muscles, and slowly releases the stress from your body with each deep breath in and out that you take. It focuses on balancing, energizing, and awakening your mind, body, and soul.

One such movement or pose in yoga known as the *Asana pose* is a good technique to adopt because it is designed to help your body achieve peace and focus through a series of movements and stretches. The movements are steady and comfortable for your body, encouraging you to be relaxed yet firm during the movement. The movements in this pose will help you greatly reduce your stress and anger levels, and it is something that you should turn to whenever you feel like you might need some calm amidst the chaotic anger in your life.

Relaxation Technique #3 – Meditation

Meditation is an experience that is truly life-changing, which in the case of learning how to manage your anger is something that you are going to need. This practice has survived for thousands of years for one very simple reason – it is *effective*. Meditation teaches you to be mindful of everything that is going on around you, to be present, and in tune with what is happening around you at this moment. Just like the other relaxation techniques above, it gives you something to focus on other than your anger. It helps you focus on the here and the now, not on what happened previously or what may happen in the near future.

Learning to meditate to relieve stress is one of the best things you can do for yourself when it comes to learning how to manage your anger and calm down. If you are a beginner to this process, opt for a guided meditation to help you transition into this practice. Guided meditation is a practice that everyone, no matter what their age, can adapt and you will find it extremely useful if you are a first-time practitioner because of the guided cues to help you along the process.

You owe it to yourself to spend a few minutes a day, every day, to start taking care of your mind, body, and soul. You've wasted so much of your energy on anger that has brought nothing beneficial to your life. It is now time that you start taking care of your body while learning effective techniques to manage your anger in the process. Meditation has proven time and time again to be one of the best tools around today to help you conquer stress and anger, and because it is so effective, this is one technique you want to keep close at hand.

Learning to Forgive

Forgiving someone who wronged you is never an easy process. In fact, for those with severe anger issues, who are capable of holding a grudge for years, this is like asking them to do the impossible. It is much easier to hold onto a grudge than it is to forgive. That's why they call forgiveness the act of *being the bigger person.* It takes great inner strength to truly forgive wholeheartedly without expecting anything in return.

Getting angry is easy. With just a snap of your fingers, you can immediately get angry. But forgiveness? That's going to take much more work. It is a skill which you must learn, similar to riding a bicycle, learning to read and write, playing the piano, or playing a sport. It is a skill that everyone has to learn because very rarely are people born with the ability to forgive as quickly as they can get angry.

One way of learning forgiveness is when you were growing up. You witnessed members of your family forgiving each other or your parents displaying acts of forgiveness. If you experienced this growing up, forgiveness might be a slightly easier task for you.

Forgiveness is something that is going to take time. It isn't going to happen overnight. That's one thing that you need to be clear about right from the beginning. Like everything else, it is a journey and the time it takes for you to reach your destination would depend entirely on your personality and how quickly you learn to adapt. The longer you hold onto a grudge or your anger, the longer the journey will be.

This part of the process will also require that you have support on your side. Because it can be so difficult and it is a process which requires great strength and courage, and even maturity on your part, the more support you have around you, the higher your chances of success will be. Do you already have a role model who is an exemplary beacon of forgiveness? Look to them for inspiration. Learn as much as you can from them, the way they forgive, and what they do to move past their anger. Tell your family and friends about what you're trying to do and let them know you would appreciate their support along the way.

Forgiveness is something that no one can force you to do. It is a choice that you alone must make. When you do choose to forgive, you must do so without expecting anything in return. Do it for your own peace of mind, not because you feel forced into it. Everything about this anger management process is about helping you regain your happiness once more and to not let anger rob you of any more joy or energy than it already has, including learning to forgive others. Do it because it is going to make things better for you and you alone.

It is also going to be a process which demands some sacrifice from you. What you would be sacrificing is:

- Your pride

- Your belief that things should always be fair to you

- Your belief that you are the victim in the situation

- Your belief that you are using your anger as a shield to protect you from even more pain

- Thinking that the other person owes you an apology before you can even consider forgiving them

- Giving up wanting revenge

- The feeling of entitlement that the other person owes you something after causing you pain and anger

- Your belief that forgiving is a sign of weakness on your part

People make mistakes. That is human nature. We hurt other people's feelings whether we intend to or not. Even you have been guilty of hurting someone else, and if they managed to forgive you, you can do the same. It is your pride and your ego that is currently standing in the way of you being able to forgive someone. However, ask yourself this: is it really worth it to be holding onto your anger? Whom is it hurting in the end?

The types of support that you can seek out, so you learn to become more forgiving, include the following:

- **Familial support** – Family is the best place to begin. Nobody will be there by your side through good times and bad the way family is. They can be your pillars of strength and provide you with the emotional support that you need when you find yourself really struggling to forgive.

- **Getting enough information** – When you've got all the information that you need, it could be of great help during the forgiveness process. Maybe you're feeling angry at a friend over an argument that you had, but you didn't realize that prior to the argument, that friend had just undergone something very stressful or something that caused them a great deal of unhappiness. Knowing the information that you didn't know makes it easier to forgive if you can empathize with them.

- **Honest feedback support** – You need people on your side who will be willing to provide you with honest feedback even at the risk of triggering your anger. This will serve as a good test for how well you're doing in terms of managing your anger when you can receive honest, constructive criticism without feeling defensive or immediately becoming angry. Honest feedback will give you a good idea of your progress, the strides you have made, and what else you need to do to improve.

Other Methods You Can Use to Help You Manage Your Anger

You always have a choice when it comes to anger. It is easy to forget that when you're so consumed by that emotion, but you do. You choose whether you want to respond or react. You choose how long you decide to hold onto your anger. You choose how much of that anger you let affect your life.

Some questions for you to ponder on include:

- Do you want to be this angry, emotional, and uncontrollable person for the rest of your life?

- Do you always want to let your emotions rule the day?

- Do you want to continue spending the rest of your life constantly apologizing for your actions and poor judgment?

- Do you want to spend the rest of your life trying to fix relationships which you damaged out of anger?

- Do you want to be judged by others? To be viewed as someone they should "stay away from" because of your bad temper?

Clearly, the answer is going to be *no,* which is why you've decided to pick up this book and find out what you can do to manage your anger in the first place. You're ready to make the necessary steps towards positive change, and that's a fantastic start!

It is now time to break your lifelong angry habits, so don't feel discouraged if you find this part of the process difficult. You've spent your entire life up until this point only knowing one way to deal and respond to your anger. Change is going to take some adjusting and getting used to, but it can be done. Now that you know the most effective relaxation techniques and that learning to forgive is part of the process, here are some other things you can do to help you manage your anger.

- **Avoid other angry people** – This one is a given. It works along the same lines as staying away from negative or toxic people if you want to achieve success in your life. If you want to learn how to become a better, less angry person, you need to stay far away from other angry people. Even if they may be your friends, this is something that must be done. If you don't keep a distance from them, they could significantly set you back in your efforts to control your anger. As much as we like to think we are strong, negative behavior patterns have a way of rubbing off on us despite our best efforts. You need to do yourself a favor and stay away from other angry people.

- **Practice patience** – This one is tricky as many angry people tend to be impatient and impulsive. You're going to have to fight all your natural instincts here and learn to exercise patience. It's not going to be easy in the beginning, but it can be done. Remind yourself that the situation you are in is not going to last forever. It isn't going to stick around and make you angry. It will come to pass, and all you have to do on your part is be patient and wait for it to fade away. Patience is not a concept that is designed to make things worse for you. Patience is a virtue. It pays to be patient, especially in anger as it can save you from many situations you might regret later.

- **By just being quiet** – When you're in an angry confrontation, the more you say, the worse things become. Once something has been said, it can never be undone, and in some cases, no amount of apologizing will be enough to remedy the situation. Why not try the opposite approach and choose to be quiet instead? Understandably, it is going to take a lot of willpower on your part, but it is much, much better than digging yourself into an even deeper hole just to satisfy the urge to say something. Whenever you're angry, put up a good fight with yourself and choose to remain quiet instead. Go off into a quiet corner or space where you can be by yourself until you have relaxed enough to come back to the situation again. It will save you much regrettable behavior in the long run.

• **Find something that makes you laugh** – Laughter truly is the best remedy for just about any situation. Whenever you feel that you need to calm down and manage your anger, find something or do something that makes you laugh. Listen to a funny story, read a joke, watch something that makes you burst with laughter and lighten your mood. Nothing cures anger faster than just having a good, hearty laugh.

Chapter 6: There Must Be Another Way – How to Solve Problems Without Anger

If you're thinking that there must be another way to solve problems without falling back on anger, you're right. There is. However, it is first going to require you to change your mindset and the way that you've been viewing the world all this time.

Angry people tend to have a very negative, pessimistic, and narrow-minded view of the world. All they see are the problems and the reasons for them to get angry. They can't see the good that is in front of them because of how their mindset is currently functioning. What you need to do right now to initiate change is to *change the way that you think.* Is it possible to change our mindset?

It is, and more importantly, it is necessary if you are ever going to see real change happening in your life. Especially if you hope to learn to control your anger issues. Our mindsets here refer to the beliefs that we have about ourselves and the qualities we possess. Some people can better control their anger than others because they have *cultivated* their mindset to become this way. People are unique individuals, and no two people are going to think, behave, or act in the same way. The difference in backgrounds, life experiences, beliefs, and situations all contribute to the kind of mindset that you have right now. If all you have been exposed to are negative mindsets, then this is all that you are going to know. It contributes to why you are an angry person.

Those who have learned to control their anger didn't manage it because they are less angry individuals. Anger is an emotion that everyone experiences – even children. The difference lies in how we each choose to respond to the anger that we experience. Steve Maraboli, the author of *The Power of One,* said that every day is a new day and it is up to you how you shape it. This statement concisely points out how much of a difference having the right mindset can have. No matter what may be happening or what situations you may be facing, it is the way that you perceive things which will make the difference. If you constantly perceive everything as situations which are only going to aggravate your anger, then that will eventually become your reality. If you believe that it is possible not to let your anger get the best of you, that it is completely possible to resolve problems without needing anger, then that will become your reality.

Our thoughts can hurt us more than we know. The problem with a negative and angry mindset is that it acts like an anchor that weighs you down, and while it may be hard to overcome, it is not impossible. To start working on improving your mindset, so you can learn how to control your anger better, here is what you need to do:

- **Believe in yourself** – If you don't believe that you are capable of change, who else will? You'll never truly achieve the level of positive mindset you hope for if you still have those nagging thoughts at the back of your mind that make you doubt if you can even pull this off. You'll never be able to become the true master of your temper if you don't first *believe that you can do it*. By believing you can achieve it, you've already put yourself one step closer to making it happen for real.

• **Be someone who is flexible** – Whenever you're angry, you can feel an overwhelmingly strong desire to want to control the situation to your advantage. You're not thinking about the other person anymore because when you're angry, it becomes all about you. Unfortunately, the reality is that you cannot always have full control and the sooner you can accept that, the faster it will be for you to build a better, healthier, and more importantly, positive frame of mind. It is time to learn to be flexible and let go, to understand that while there may be some things which are beyond your control, one thing you do have control over is how *not to respond in anger*.

• **Keep only positive people in your circle** – Stay away from the rageaholics but keep the ones who radiate with positivity close to you. This is how to learn to see things from a better perspective, to improve your mindset by emulating those who have already done it. Negative and angry people will only weigh you down just like anchors. Even worse, they will rub off on you and make it impossible to get your anger management under control. When you surround yourself with only people with positive mindsets, you'll slowly adapt the way you think to emulate them as their wisdom, their outlook, stories, and affirmations slowly seep into your way of thinking.

• **Build up your resilience** – Having a better mindset will involve you working on building up your resilience. This means that you will have to become a more determined individual, no longer let challenges and setbacks affect you mentally and emotionally, and keep persisting even when things are difficult. Building up your resilience until you are a stronger person mentally and emotionally will help you control your anger in a way that you were never able to before.

• **Get a mantra** – It's not different from having positive affirmations. Having a personal mantra is something that will empower you and remind you to be optimistic each time you find yourself face-to-face with another challenge. A mantra like *I am the one in control, not my anger* or *I will not let my anger get the best of me today!* is good enough to start. A mantra can be anything that you want. It is entirely up to you. All you have to do is pick one that makes you feel empowered enough to change your mindset. Repeat it over and over again until you find your mindset shifting in the direction that you want it to go.

•**The mirror technique** – This technique is a great one for exercising change for your mindset. Whenever you look at your reflection in the mirror each morning, say something positive. Tell yourself, for example, *I am not someone who is ruled by anger.* Be genuine and believe every word that you say. Say each word with conviction while you look yourself in the eye. You could also repeat your mantra this way. Keep up this habit, and soon it will become an effortless exercise as your mindset improves.

You Also Need to Understand Your Anger

You need to understand your anger before you can learn to manage it. How would you manage something that you don't fully understand? Which is why it is so important to analyze the feelings that you have, dissect them and get to the root of the problem, and ask yourself how you could respond better in the situation.

Here are a couple of crucial questions that you need to start thinking about in times of anger:

•**Who am I angry at? Really?** – Although your first instinct may be to immediately point the finger at the person who provoked your anger, pause for a moment and look a little deeper. Is this really the case? Or were you already carrying around pent-up anger that you may not have realized and the person just happened to say or do something that triggered it? It is easy to immediately point the blame at whatever seems to be the most convenient, but if you want to learn how to solve problems without anger, you need to start looking a little deeper. Things may not always be what they seem.

• **Is this the right time or place to get angry?** – There is a time, and a place, for everything, including managing your moments of anger. For example, having an explosive episode right in the middle of your office in front of your boss or manager is not the right time or place. Letting your temper fly in the middle of the supermarket aisle is not the right time or place. The thing about anger is it can sometimes crop up at the most inconvenient of times. To learn how to start solving problems without anger, always stop and ask yourself, *Is this the right time or place to get angry*? If you know it is inappropriate, then don't do it.

• **Exactly *why* am I angry?** – You may have been angry for so long that it seems like second nature to you. You don't even know *why* you're angry anymore. Think of a time where you argued with a friend or family member, and the two of you ended up not speaking for years. The problem seems to have faded away as you went about your daily lives. When someone asks what happened between the two of you, you find yourself lost for words because you can't exactly remember why you were so angry in the first place or what the argument was even about. That happens when you let your anger drag on for so long. You've forgotten what the underlying issue really was. There is always a better way to resolve problems without having to resort to anger, but it first requires that you *understand why on earth* you were so angry in the first place? If it wasn't worth it, then why do it?

• **Is the consequence worth it?** – For every action, there is an equal and opposite reaction. This is Newton's infamous third law of physics, and it's very applicable to moments of anger. Everything that you do in anger has a price and a consequence which follows. Each time you feel yourself about to fly off the handle, you need to stop and ask yourself if the price you have to pay for this brief moment of satisfaction is going to be worth it. Is it worth ruining relationships? Is it worth causing even bigger problems later on? Is it worth damaging your reputation over? Is it worth wasting your energy on? Don't forget that things said in anger can never be unsaid. Once it's out there, there's no taking it back. The moment you say something hurtful in anger, that you wish you could take back, is the moment that it may be too late.

Now, What are My Options to Resolve Problems Without Anger

It is always up to you to choose how you would like to respond. There is no hard and fast rule that the only acceptable response to situations which incite you is anger. Anger, in fact, should be a last resort, even better if you don't have to resort to anger at all. The question is, *how do you want to resolve the problem?* You have an infinite number of options depending on the time, place, circumstance, and the present situation. However, at the end of the day, the choice remains yours.

Some strategies to keep in mind on how to resolve problems without having to resort to anger are:

• **Forget about exercise** – Exercising your right to be angry that is. You may feel that you are entitled to that moment of anger because this person or situation has wronged you, but that is exactly how *not* to keep your anger under control. Want to resolve problems without resorting to anger? Forget about your right to be angry.

• **Learn to listen actively** – If you're in an argument with someone, learn to listen actively to what it is they're saying. Listening and listening actively are two different things. The latter will help you to empathize more with the person you're in an argument with and see where they are coming from. This, in turn, will help to minimize the possibility of the argument escalating to the point that you will both regret later on. Listening actively means being mindful of everything the other person is saying. You're making a conscious effort to actively receive and process the information that is being given to you, and you're able to connect with what's being said, reflect on the information, and finally be able to provide constructive, thoughtful and proactive responses because of it. By listening actively, you will see that every problem can be resolved amicably and there is no real reason to bring anger into the mix at all.

• **Always check in with your emotions** – This is where being mindful again comes into play. No matter what situation you find yourself in, always remember to stop and check in with yourself. How are you feeling? Are you all right? How does this person or situation make you feel right now? If you feel yourself getting irritated or stressed, what can you do about it? Close your eyes and take a couple of measured deep breaths, remind yourself to focus on your present, and shift your mind away from what is threatening to trigger your anger. Remind yourself that you *want to resolve problems without the need for anger*.

•**You don't need the last word** – Resist the urge to have the final say. It is not always about you. The constant need to be right, to always have the last word just to quench your satisfaction and ego is exactly how anger makes problems and arguments much worse. If you want to resolve problems without having to resort to anger, learn to swallow your pride and resist the urge to fight back. Resist the urge to counter what someone else is saying with another defensive argument of your own. That does nothing to help the situation.

• **Talk about your feelings** – Before you begin to get angry, try talking about your feelings beforehand. If you know you are about to have an unpleasant conversation with someone, start by saying, "I know we need to talk about this and this is the way I'm feeling right now." Explain your position in a calm, controlled manner in a neutral tone of voice that does not imply you are blaming or accusing the other person of anything. Being able to verbalize your feelings instead of jumping headfirst into the situation is how you keep anger out of the equation. By talking about your feelings beforehand, the other person will right away be able to see where you are coming from and how you already feel before the discussion.

• **No judgments please** – If you go into a conversation with an already preconceived notion in mind or even prejudice, that is just an argument waiting to happen. Although yes, admittedly, we have all been guilty of being critical or judgmental. This is not the best approach to use if you are hoping to resolve problems without anger. You need to leave your judgments and criticism at the door where they belong and don't bring them into the conversation or situation you may currently be engaged in. Being overly critical is how you put yourself at risk of making potentially snarky or sarcastic comments which could aggravate the situation and cause an argument. That is how you learn how to resolve problems without the need for anger.

• **No more blame** – It is time to stop the blame game once and for all. If you're always looking for an opportunity to blame someone else, to eagerly shift the blame, so you end up looking like "the good one", how do you ever hope to resolve conflict without having to resort to anger? Always looking for a chance to blame someone else is a sign of someone with low emotional intelligence, an individual who is toxic and difficult to be around. Don't be this person because you know you are capable of being so much better than that. Enough with the blame game; it is time to toss that aside and start focusing on resolving problems like a mature individual.

• **Ditch the negative mindset** – A negative mind will be able to see nothing but problems in front of them. It is almost like negativity somehow blinds you to the opportunities and the other options which are in front of you. There could be a dozen other pathways which you could take to avoid anger in that situation, but if you're always harping on the negative, you won't be able to see any of those things. All you would be able to think about is how bad and how unfair everything is, or how angry this person is making you right now.

Chapter 7: Avoid & Escape – Catching Anger Before It Hits at Home, Work and Public Arenas

At home. At work. In a public arena.

These are the three main areas where you should strive to focus on managing your temper the most. Home and work especially are the two main areas that you are going to spend the most time every day. When you're not at home, you're at work. When you're not at work, you're often at home or in a public area. Therefore, it is only fitting that you put your best effort forward when it comes to managing your anger within these three areas.

What you want to do right now is to try and avoid and keep your anger from surfacing altogether by catching that emotion and doing something about it before it starts to take over. You are trying to be the one in control right now.

Catching Anger Before It Hits at Home

Your home is where you feel comfortable, free to be yourself. It's your safe space and your sanctuary. Which is why sometimes we don't even think twice about trying to control our anger when we're in our homes; we just let it fly. Only later do we realize that maybe we shouldn't have done that. We're not as controlled as we are at home around family because we assume that they already know this is who we are and they have to accept it whether they like it or not. Because they're family.

However, this is not the right way to think at all. Just because they are your family, it doesn't mean they are without feelings. They can get just as hurt by your words and actions as strangers or friends do. Just because they are family, it doesn't automatically mean they have to put up with everything and not feel any pain when you hurt them or that saying sorry is going to make everything okay, like nothing happened.

Family is the very reason *why* you should try so hard to control and manage your anger. These are people that you love, people who mean more to you than anyone else in the world. They are the people who are worth fighting for, and you should put up a good fight against your anger, starting in your home.

To start catching anger in your home before it gets out of control, here is what you can start doing:

> • **Always choose to respond kindly** – It can be easy to lash back when a family member confronts you angrily or does something that aggravates you enough to the point of anger. For example, teenagers drive their parents crazy with their attitude at times and when that happens, what do the parents do? Automatically the parents will jump into the argument because they are feeling annoyed already and if the situation continues, both parties could end up in a heated argument with each other. What should you do in a situation like this? Always choose to be kind and empathize. Remember that this is a person you love and getting angry is simply not worth the time, energy, and effort. There are always other ways to resolve conflict which don't have to involve arguments all

the time. Let love be the reason that you choose to respond kindly.

• **Choose to set a good example** – This is especially important if you have children of your own at home. The last kind of role model that you want to be is that of an angry parent. Do you want your kids growing up to become somebody who lashes out in anger all the time? Someone whom other people view as toxic individuals because they can't keep their temper under control? Children learn first and foremost by the example that you set for them, and if you are a parent who always gives into your angry desires, rants, shouts, raves, curses, and even hits family members in anger, this is what they will be observing. This is what they will grow up knowing, and without even realizing it, they'll be emulating your behavior. For the sake of your children, choose to set a good example. Lead by example and let the example be that there is always another way to resolve the conflict, which does not have to end in an angry argument. As a parent, you will be the one who sets the tone at home. What kind of tone do you want to set? One of harmony and love? Or one of anger?

• **Be open to conversation** – Don't be dismissive of another family member's concerns, unhappiness, or opinions. Don't be dismissive of conflicts because avoiding them is only going to make things much worse. Whenever there is a problem, you need to address it before it escalates and festers into an even bigger problem which may result in an angry shouting match between one, two, or several family members. What you are trying to do is learn how to catch and manage your anger at home before it can even hit, so if you see a concern or a possible conflict in the making, suggest that those involved sit down and have a heart-to-heart discussion about it. All conflicts can be resolved. We just have to make an effort to try. Be comfortable talking about what makes you angry. It is nothing to be ashamed of. Talking about it is much better than showing it.

• **Don't use anger as a form of punishment** – If you're guilty of giving family members the silent treatment for days or even weeks because you're angry, it is time to stop. That's not catching your anger; that's you giving in to your anger and choosing to wallow in it instead of finding constructive ways to resolve that anger. Ask yourself this, *What good is punishing them with my anger doing except creating disharmony and unhappiness in the family?* The answer will be nothing. Nothing good is going to come out of it. You're just going to cause many people to be unhappy and feel sad. It may give you a sense of satisfaction knowing you're inflicting this kind of emotional pain on others because you are feeling so angry, but it isn't worth it. These are people you love. What you should do is treat them with nothing but love and respect in return.

Catching Anger Before It Hits at Work

Anger at work could begin in the subtle form of a disgruntled employee. *You* could be that unhappy employee and the little things that start to aggravate you are slowly building up inside. You feel like you could be on the verge of exploding.

Some signs to look out for to identify if you or another employee is potentially feeling unhappy at work include:

- Losing interest in work.

- Becoming disagreeable. Everything is not right no matter what is said.

- Becoming antisocial by barely engaging with team members or other colleagues anymore.

- Becoming snappy when someone attempts to start a conversation.

- Appearing distracted and unfocused on work duties.

- Displaying a lack of respect for team members, maybe even superiors.

- Taking more sick days and finding excuses to stay away from work.

- No longer interested in giving 100% effort towards the company.

- Becoming vocal about dissatisfaction.

Do these signs sound relatable? Do you know someone within your workplace that might be he harboring some anger under the surface? Maybe you are feeling all these emotions, and you're just trying to keep your anger bottled in, but it's getting harder to control. The good news is you now know how to recognize these signs so that you can put a stop to it before your anger erupts at work. Maybe you could even offer to help out that disgruntled coworker so that *their* temper doesn't unleash.

To catch anger at work before it escalates into something unpleasant, here is what you need to do:

- **Learn to accept reality** – You may not be entirely happy with the way things are done in the company, but making major changes that better suit your needs is not your decision to make. Unless the company is yours of course. You always have a choice to leave and look for work elsewhere if being there is truly making you unhappy and irritable, but if you decide to stay, you need to accept the good and the bad about the job and face reality. If you notice your coworker feeling this way, offer to catch up over a chat and have a talk about it. Empathize with them. Tell them you understand how they feel because sometimes you feel the same way. Point out that there are options and it is up to them what they want to do. If you or your coworker decides to stay, then you need to learn to accept the reality that things are the way they are. They may change, or they may not, but there is no sense in getting all angry and worked up about it.

• **Don't take it personally** – The company's issues are not about you. You may not like the company's policy, but it isn't about you. You may not like the way certain things are done, but again it is not about you. The more you take things personally like there's a personal vendetta against you, the unhappier you are going to be. Some of your other coworkers may be just as unhappy about a policy or the way things are done, but they're not taking it personally and internalizing all that frustration until it becomes anger. Neither should you. It isn't about you; it's just business. Remember that if you don't like it, you always have a choice to seek employment elsewhere.

• **Take a step back** – Do you feel like you are working far too much and not being adequately rewarded for your efforts? The lack of recognition starts to aggravate you? Then take a step back and slow it down a little instead of getting all worked up about it. Simple, easy to resolve matters like these are just not worth wasting all your energy getting angry about. If your employer is not demanding that you work overtime for example, but you choose to do it anyway in the hopes of getting a big pay rise later, this was your decision to make. Nobody forced you into it, so don't be disgruntled and unhappy when you feel you are not being adequately rewarded. You always have a choice to take a step back and slow it down a little if it's getting to be too much.

• **Mingle with upbeat coworkers** – Not every employee is going to be as dissatisfied or unhappy with the company that they are working in. If you're working for a big organization, you will find lots of different personalities coming together under one roof. Seek out employees who have a positive outlook, who come to work with a smile on their face and a spring in their step, always looking forward to a brand-new day. Let their optimism rub off on you and help alleviate some of that pent-up frustration you've been feeling. Remember how in the earlier chapters we talked about keeping the right kind of company? This is something that you need to do at work too. Avoid colleagues who are just as unhappy and as miserable as you feel because getting together will only serve to fuel your feelings of dissatisfaction. What you're trying to do is put a stop to it before your anger can get the best of you at work, so you need to do the complete opposite and mingle with coworkers who can lift your spirits instead.

• **Look for the good in your job** – There must be at least one thing about your job that you're good at. Or something that makes you happy enough. Is it the flexible work hours? A good superior that you can talk to and who understands? Maybe the coworker in the next cubicle who never fails to make you laugh? Are you good at several aspects of your job which gives you a sense of accomplishment when you do it? Focus on the good things that you have to look forward to, instead of focusing on all the things which are making you grumpy and irritable at work. Make the positive aspects your primary focus. Each time that you feel yourself getting angry or feeling unhappy at work think about the good things about your job that you can look forward to each day. Think about it this way too: if your job really was that terrible, why are you still in it instead of looking for opportunities elsewhere?

Catching Anger Before It Hits at Public Arenas

In public we are, generally, on our best behavior because we are conscious of other people being around us. However, sometimes a moment of anger can strike, and you forget all about being out in public and just let your anger fly. It happens to the best of us. But all hope is not lost. There are still strategies and tools which you can use to help you catch your anger before it hits in public arenas.

• **Be more tolerant** – You are out and about in the world, and you have to share this world that we live in with millions of other people. Unlike your home, this is not a place where you can have things done your way. Or expect things to be done your way. It isn't about you when it comes to a public space; it is about everyone. If you choose to be intolerant and let the little things get to you, you're going to find it very challenging to keep your cool in public. You need to become a more tolerant person by accepting that you're not entitled to anything, and people are not here to conform to what you want. Just like how everyone else is tolerant about what you do in public, you need to show that same respect towards them. If you don't like something, there's always a choice to walk away and remove yourself from the situation.

• **Again, don't take it personally** – Just like at work, don't take it personally. Other people are just going about their business in public like you are. They are not there to purposely go out of their way to irritate or aggravate you. If you observe someone doing or saying something which starts to trigger your anger, remove yourself from the situation. You have a choice about it. You don't need to take it personally because this person is a complete stranger to you. Why should they purposely be doing something that annoys you?

• **Be polite and courteous** – The use of expletives these days happens all too frequently. It has become second nature to many of us to swear when things are not going our way. However, using an expletive in a public space could sometimes result in a case of saying something at the wrong time in the wrong place. This could then potentially lead to an argument because something you said angered someone else, who took it personally or misunderstood it. There are so many things which could go wrong in a situation like this, so if you want to do everything that you can to catch your anger and manage it within a public setting, you can start by doing the simple thing – be polite and courteous at all times whenever you're out in public.

• **Settle for being annoyed and walk away** – You don't have to allow yourself to reach a point of uncontrollable anger when you're out in public. Sometimes, certain circumstances may be unavoidable, and somehow, despite your best efforts, you find yourself in a situation that is causing (or going to cause you) a great deal of anger. How about a compromise instead? If you want to manage your anger better, learn to settle for just being annoyed or irritated and then immediately walk away or remove yourself from the situation. Don't stick around until your irritation escalates into something more. Being annoyed is also much easier to overcome and get over than anger. The next time that you find yourself in a situation that is inciting your anger try to keep things in perspective. Be annoyed but then make that the limit. There is no reason to take it any further. It is not the end of the world. Once again, don't take it personally. Settle for being annoyed and then walk away.

Chapter 8: Three Devils – The Relationship among Anger, Stress, and Anxiety

Anger, stress, and anxiety. Possibly the worst trifecta you could have. The three often run so closely together and the emotions become interchangeable that it is sometimes hard to tell where one ends and the other begins. Anger could be triggered by stress, stress could be triggered by anxiety, and anxiety could make way for anger which then leads to even more stress. Too much stress in your life could also cause anxiety and anger issues.

In this chapter, we will be exploring stress and anxiety in further detail and the link between those two emotions and how they could contribute to your anger issues.

Distinguishing Stress from the Rest

As the world continues to progress at a faster and faster pace, so do our stress levels because of our non-stop, hectic, and on the go lifestyles. Stress has become a normal part of our everyday living. The early humans also felt stress, but not in the same way that we do today. Their version of stress was what activated their fight or flight response when they had to survive in the wilderness. It helped them survive and stay alive. It helped them hunt, respond quickly when danger was present, and it is a very large part of why the human race is still going strong today.

When you think about the word stress, what image springs to mind? Or what do you associate with the term stress? Something that is bad for you? Something that wreaks havoc in your life and on your health? Something that causes you constant headaches? Stress has certainly got a bad reputation for itself because of the negative connotations associated with it.

As much as we would like it to be so, it's almost impossible to feel happy-go-lucky and carefree all the time. You can try your best to remain positive and optimistic each day, but there will be an occasion or several where you may feel stress knocking at your door. If only things could run smoothly all the time. That's where stress comes into play. There are two types of stress, and we ordinarily deal with one good and one bad.

Good stress can be beneficial and can even motivate you to perform better than you ordinarily would. The bad stress is the one that is associated with anxiety, possibly causing depression if it is experienced at a chronic level and a whole host of other health-related problems. The bad stress is the one that contributes and even triggers our anger.

What happens to your body when you typically feel stressed include:

- Pupil dilation

- Blood pressure levels rise

- Your heart rate increases

- Your breathing quickens

- Your muscles feel tense and tight especially around your shoulders

- Adrenaline starts pumping through your body which is why you often feel a sudden "surge" or "rush"

- You start sweating profusely, especially on your palms

- Your cortisol levels increase

There's a lot that can happen to your body when you're feeling stressed. No wonder it is such a draining emotion, just like anger is. As with your anger, stress can be caused by several factors, and it would help you to begin identifying what the cause of your stress is.

Some examples of stress triggers could include situations, circumstances, certain people, events, your job, deadlines, traffic, an emotional situation, relationships, heartbreak, death, starting a new phase in life, sudden change, and more. Stress can be caused by a wide variety of factors and differs between individuals. What is a stress trigger for one person may not be one for someone else.

Stress can be categorized into two types. One is major stress triggers, and the other is minor stress triggers. Some examples of major stress triggers include the following:

- Contracting a chronic illness

- Being fired from your job

- Being yelled at by your boss

- Financial matters

- Having big bills to pay each month

- Experiencing death

- Having a major life change happen

Some examples of minor stress triggers include:

- When you're rushing to meet a deadline

- When you're hurrying to meet a friend or an appointment, and you're at risk of running late

- Being disturbed when you're in the middle of something

- Heavy traffic and rush hour

- When someone has taken one of your things without permission and used it

- Looking after a sick family member

- Rushing from one task to the next

- When you've misplaced something important

- When someone is running late to an appointment you set up

- Meeting difficult clients

Each person would have a different tolerance for stress. Some people can handle large amounts of stress well and still maintain a cool head on their shoulders. Others, who don't cope with stress as well, end up tense, frustrated, and – you guessed it – angry. While bad stress in small doses is still manageable, there are certain types of stress which are bordering on toxic. The toxic stress is the one you want to stay away from because it does nothing to help try and manage your anger issues.

The toxic types of stress include the following:

- ***The type of stress that is cumulative***

This type of stress tends to accumulate over time (just like your anger does). When things pile on top of each other, your stress tends to grow and build like a snowball, until one day, it bursts forth either in the form of anger or anxiety. This usually happens when you reach a point where you can't take it anymore, and everything just feels like it is getting out of hand.

- ***The type of stress that is chronic***

This type of stress just always seems to hang around you and never fully goes away. It can be very toxic because it means you find yourself in a constant state of unhappiness, feel nervous or anxious, and always jumpy like you are just waiting for the next thing to go wrong in your life. It can also manifest itself as a chronic anger because you become snappy, irritable and you find it difficult to concentrate on any of the tasks that you're supposed to be doing.

Is this Anxiety? Or am I Just a Stressed-out Person?

Anxiety can sometimes be hard to distinguish from stress, especially if you don't know for sure that you may be dealing with anxiety in the first place. Ask yourself these questions for a moment:

- Do you find yourself feeling constantly tense and on edge all the time?

- Do your worries make you so fearful that it is all you can think about?

- Is what you are worried about starting to prevent you from running your daily routine normally because you're so worked up by it?

- Do those nagging thoughts just never seem to leave you?

If your worries are more than just temporary, sometimes bordering on fear, and they bother you more often than they should, you could be dealing with more than just stress. You could be dealing with anxiety.

Anxiety is a combination of several different factors which contribute to this emotion. It is the human body's natural response to stress. According to the American Psychological Association (APA), anxiety is an emotion which is characterized by feelings that include worried thoughts, tension, and even physical changes in the body, such as an increase in blood pressure. It is hard to pinpoint exactly what the causes of anxiety are because there are so many factors which could contribute towards a person experiencing anxiety. It is unique to each person, what they are going through, and what they may have experienced in the past.

While it is hard to determine for sure what could cause someone to experience anxiety, there are several examples that we could look at for possible situations where a person's anxiety might be triggered. These situations include:

•**You fear rejection** – If you are someone who suffers from low self-esteem, having a fear of rejection is something which could potentially cause you to feel anxious. This is because you already have a low opinion of yourself. This low self- esteem is what is going to feed into your anxiety about being rejected by the people around you. The only thing you can think about is your flaws, and you can't comprehend why other people want to be around you in the first place. So you end up worrying and obsessing possibly every waking moment that one day you find yourself all alone with nobody to turn to, especially because of your issues with anxiety.

• **You fear to be alone** – Linked to the point above, a fear of being alone is also a possible cause for anxiety. Nobody ever really wants to be alone. Some people do enjoy the occasional solitude but being completely and utterly alone in this world is not something that anybody wants. Human beings are social creatures, and we crave intimacy and a connection with other human beings. Even the introverts. Dealing with anxiety, you constantly worry about being alone. You worry that your anxiety makes people turn away from you and they will not be able to love you for who you are because you've forgotten your own self-worth. You worry all the time, and one of your worst fears is that the people that love you will eventually give up on you because your anxiety becomes too much for them.

• **You fear change in your life** – Some people adapt and adjust well to the changes they experience in their life.

Others, not so much. When major change takes place, it is normal to feel concerned about how everything is going to go, if things are going to work out for the best. If you are dealing with anxiety, this can be a trigger because anxiety causes you to be resistant to change. You're afraid of what is going to happen when things change, and you worry about whether you will be able to cope. What if you have a complete nervous breakdown? What is going to happen if you hate the new change that's taking place in your life? Anxiety can make it difficult for those who have it to be receptive to change, and they may take longer than usual to adapt and adjust to the new situations or surroundings that they are faced with.

How Do I Manage My Anxiety?

Nobody likes having anxious thoughts that disrupt their everyday routine. It's hard to function when all you can think about is your worries and what could go wrong at every turn. It is even worse when they become so bad that it causes you immense amounts of stress, which then leads to anger because the pressure just feels like it is too much to bear. Living with anxiety may not be easy, but at least there is something you can do about it.

The following strategies will help you manage and keep your anxiety in check, so you can then learn to manage your stress and anger much better.

• **Question yourself** – Or rather, your thoughts whenever they pop up and threaten to jumpstart your anxiety and make you stressed. Whenever you start having an anxious thought, stop and ask yourself why this is happening? What is the root cause of that worry and is it justifiable to worry this much about it? Look for your triggers and identify what is making you feel this way. Ask yourself if you are worrying for nothing. Or do you have tangible facts to go on? Take a moment to question your worry and work through whether this is something that you should get anxious over or not.

• **Identifying your triggers** – Just like the other two emotions, you need to apply that same process here. Everyone has different anxiety triggers, and it is important to learn what yours are. What is causing you to feel anxious right now? Is it something that you're dealing with at work or in your personal life? What about your relationships? Are you currently going through something stressful which causes anxious thoughts? Identifying your triggers will give you a better handle at controlling your anxiety because you will come to know what to expect and you'll be able to take the necessary pre-emptive measures to prepare for it.

• **Ensure that you're getting a good night's sleep** – It is often underestimated how important getting a good night sleep is. It is such a simple yet effective tool which unfortunately most people do not follow enough. Feeling anxious all the time can cause you to feel drained and fatigued, two emotions that stop you from performing or going through the day at your fullest potential. When you're in this state, you're unable to focus or think as clearly as you should. Situations and circumstances which are manageable somehow suddenly seem like an impossible task to overcome. Start making it a habit to always get a good night's sleep each night with the recommended number of hours, so you're always feeling your best. It'll help to keep your stress and anger under control too.

• **Keep a thought journal** – Now, before you dismiss this and say journaling or writing is not something for you, consider the benefits first. Often, our anxious thoughts and worries can seem magnified and worse than they should when they're bottled up inside our minds with no escape outlet. This is how it leads to stress and unchecked anger because we're not coping and dealing with it properly the way that we should.

This is why keeping a thought journal is going to be so useful. Whenever you're feeling anxious or an anxious thought is nagging you, pour it all out onto your journal. Instead of unleashing all that pent-up emotion in the form of anger against someone else, isn't it better to let it out in your journal where no one gets hurt? Your journal is for you and you alone. Be free and pour your heart and soul into it. Nobody is going to judge you for it. Nobody will even see your innermost thoughts. It is a private space for you and you alone to process and work through everything that you're feeling.

• **Lean on those you can trust** – Don't be afraid to ask for help when something seems too overwhelming. Going through a challenge always feels more manageable when you've got someone you can trust to help you through it. It makes a world of difference when you're dealing with it on your own and when you have the proper support system in place. This could be all it takes to mean the difference between successfully managing your anxiety, stress and anger, and failure to do so. Find a circle of people – friends or family – that you trust completely to be there for you and lean on them for support.

• **Be patient with yourself** – If only getting rid of anxiety were that simple. We would all like to toss our anxieties out the window and get rid of them just like that. Unfortunately, it isn't quite as simple as that. Just like overcoming and learning how to manage your anger, there is no magic formula, no shortcut to the process, no overnight solution that is going to work miracles. Overcoming anxiety is a process which takes time, and you need to prepare yourself for that to avoid frustrations along the way. Start small by making little daily goals for yourself to help you overcome your anxious thoughts over time and eventually with each little success, your confidence will grow as you get better at taking control over your anxiety.

If despite using the methods above, you are still having a very difficult time coping and managing your anxiety, you would need to consider getting treatments to help you overcome these emotions. The following examples are instances of when you should consider getting a medical opinion for your anxiety issues:

- When you have reason to believe that an underlying medical condition is causing your anxiety.

- When your anxiety is causing you to have suicidal thoughts and a tendency to inflict self-harm.

- When you feel like your anxieties are too much to bear, and they are still out of control despite your best efforts at managing them.

- When going through and functioning each day becomes too difficult to do anymore.

- When you feel the urge to turn towards substances like drugs or alcohol to help you cope with your anxiety.

If at any point you are genuinely concerned about your health and wellbeing, you should seek the advice of a medical professional immediately. Anxiety could lead to other serious medical conditions if not treated properly and we're not talking about just anger and stress-related issues anymore.

Chapter 9: When it isn't you – How to Deal with Angry People

Sometimes it's you, and sometimes it isn't. There could be times when *your* anger is not the problem. It's not you; it's them. It seems like a lot, doesn't it? Having to manage your anger issues *and* learning how to deal with angry people on top of that.

How do you deal with angry people without running the risk of losing your temper and still resolving the situation in responding and reacting appropriately to reach an amicable resolution? Through communication.

In times of anger, there is a distinctive communication breakdown, especially when both people engaged in a confrontation are angry individuals who have lost control of their emotions. Communication is a complex matter as it is whether in everyday life or at work. When you're dealing with it in anger, it becomes even more complex. Misinterpretations can cause even more anger. Messages that don't come across clearly cause even more anger and frustration on both parts.

Some of the common communication barriers which are likely to occur when you're dealing with one or several angry individuals include the following:

- **Making assumptions** – This is a dangerous one when you're dealing with angry individuals. Making assumptions is a common communication barrier, and this frequently occurs when someone decides to reach a decision or course of action without fully listening to all the information at hand. Do you see why active listening is such an important skill to have when it comes to learning how to manage anger? Making assumptions can lead to complications because when you are not well informed, you run the risk of making more mistakes than you should. By assuming you know how the person is thinking, feeling, or what they mean by their actions, you run the risk of making the situation much worse.

- **Not giving your full attention** – Not giving your full attention to the person who is speaking to you is considered a communication barrier. If you were the angry party who was trying to convey your message and you noticed that the other person was not giving you their full attention, what do you think would happen? Chances are you'd probably get even angrier. Admittedly, yes, sometimes, our mind tends to wander or drift when someone else is talking. When attention starts to drift, it can be easy to miss crucial points in the message, and when you're dealing with an angry person, it is even more important than ever to pay attention to detail if you want to maintain any hopes of resolving the situation amicably.

- **Using expletives or jargon** – Using expletives is a definite *no* when it comes to trying to diffuse an angry situation. Even if you feel like you may be on the verge of not being able to hold back any longer, tap into your willpower a little bit more and just don't do it. Also, using jargons can be a communication barrier too in a situation like this. Not everyone may be familiar with certain jargons, and sometimes these unfamiliar terms can cause confusion and complicate things for the person who is trying to understand your message. In an angry situation, not being able to understand might cause even more frustration, irritation, and anger.

- **Saying too much at once** – In their anger, a person may be rushing through their message, trying to get everything out there in the open. Making it clear how angry they may be feeling. Or, in your attempt to try and calm the person down, you could be the one rushing through your message trying to make yourself heard. One thing that everyone would do well to remember when it comes to communication is that not everyone thinks, reacts, or processes information in the same way. One person may be able to process information quickly and efficiently, while someone else may need more time to digest that same piece of information properly. This can prove to be a hindrance when you're trying to deal with an angry individual because you could risk just aggravating them even more. If they feel frustrated at not being able to understand what you're saying, that will only serve to fuel their anger even more. Delivering too much too soon runs the risk of overwhelming the receiver, and as a result, they may not be able to fully process or understand what it is that you're trying to convey. Misunderstandings can often occur in this case, which may lead to – you guessed it – even more anger. In this scenario, it may be best just to let them do all the talking first before you speak up and say anything.

How to Deal with Angry People

To learn how to manage someone else's anger, so it doesn't rub off on you and threaten to derail your attempts at managing your anger, use the following guidelines to help you.

- **Focus on the problem at hand** – It can be hard to lose sight of what you should be focusing on when you're dealing with someone who is threatening to raise your anger to the surface, but it is important that you remain calm in this situation. Focus on dealing with the problem at hand and not the angry person that is in front of you. It is easy to feel like the angry person is personally attacking you, but if you get to the root of the problem, you'll find that is not always the case.

- **Be the cool cucumber in this case** – This can be a very difficult thing to do, admittedly, but *someone* has got to keep a cool head. Otherwise, the argument could get really ugly. That is the last thing that you want, where the two of you end up in a shouting match against one another, possibly saying things which can never be taken back. Tap into every ounce of willpower that you have to remain the one who stays calm in this situation. Remember that this person is going through the same thing that you are. You were once in a position where you had a lot of trouble learning how to control and manage your anger. Empathize and see things from their point of view. Be the bigger person that encourages them to remain calm and remind them to calm down and resolve the problem in a more civilized manner. Don't internalize their anger and make it your own; remember, it may not be about you at all. They're just having trouble properly channeling their anger in the right way.

- **Keep your tone polite and civil** – It can be very easy to fall into the trap of shouting back to defend yourself when someone is yelling at you. However, this, of course, is the last thing that you should do. What you should do instead is to keep your tone polite and civil throughout the conversation, regardless of the way that the other person is acting. When you're angry, the way that you say things and your tone of voice can incite just as much anger as the words that you say. When you keep your tone civil, there is a much higher chance that the other person will calm down and start to lower their tone of voice too when they see that you're not yelling back at them. It can be very humbling for the angry person, and it may just make them stop and think twice about the way they are acting.

• **Always be respectful** – Even if the other person is not. The way they behave is not your responsibility. You are responsible for your actions, and you should do everything that you can to ensure you don't do anything that you will only regret later on. Maintain respectful behavior throughout the conversation, and this will reflect on your maturity. It will also say a lot about how far you have come in terms of your anger management attempts. Under no circumstance during a confrontation with another angry individual should you roll your eyes, display sarcasm, make snide remarks that will only incite them further, point blame, lecture, criticize, or use foul language.

• **Ask for a timeout if you need it** – You have every right to ask for one if you feel the situation calls for it. Walk away and come back to the conversation later when you've got a much clearer head and the other person has had some time to calm down. This is especially important if you're finding it harder to control your levels of anger at this point, and instead of running the risk of letting your temper fly, take a timeout. Speak up and let the other person know that you feel this would be better discussed at a more appropriate time. If they disagree, be firm about it and request that they respect your decision.

• **Clarify and confirm** – Angry people want to be heard and understood. They want others to know why they are feeling the way that they are, what's upsetting them, and why they are so frustrated. To help diffuse the situation and come to an amicable agreement or solution, spend some time clarifying and ensuring that you understood what they were trying to say. Also, make sure that they understood what *you* are trying to say. To help you determine if your message is clear enough, ask yourself if the objective of the message is clear and if you are getting all the important information across. Let them know that you hear what they are saying and you're doing your best to try and help them solve the problem.

• **Using the right words** – This is just as important as watching the tone of your voice. Sometimes all it takes is for someone just to say one wrong thing to make a bad situation worse. Word selection is important in determining how effective your messages come across. Words are the source of facilitating effective communication, and careless or improper use of words are usually the reason for misplaced anger. In an attempt to try and effectively handle difficult individuals, think about using the right types of words when you're in a conversation with them. Opt for common and familiar words, single words which deliver the point across more concisely instead of several words. Use shorter words where possible. Speak succinctly and clearly. The more concise and succinct your message, the easier it is to understand, and the less chance there is for misunderstandings to occur.

• **Don't appear superior** – While you may be the bigger person in this situation and the one who is trying to keep the peace, avoid inflicting an air of superiority when dealing with an angry individual. You'll have a better chance of effectively dealing with them if you are relatable. Talk to them like an equal because this helps them be more receptive and attentive to the things you have to say, even when they are angry.

Learning How to Communicate Properly with Angry Individuals

Now that we have established the importance of communication when dealing with an angry individual, here comes the next question – how do you work on improving your communication skills so you can effectively deal with angry individuals? You have your own anger management issues to contend with, and that is already a lot to deal with. Dealing with other angry individuals may be aggravating to you because it makes it harder to keep a firm control of your temper. However, communicating with them well, making yourself understood *and understanding them* is essential if you hope to resolve an angry situation as peacefully as possible.

In a situation like this, both your verbal and non-verbal skills are going to come into play. It is not just about the way that you speak, but also the manner in which you carry yourself that makes you an effective communicator overall. For example, if you were to come off with an aggressive body stance, an angry expression on your face, and arms folded in front of your chest, what kind of message does that send to the other person? If they were already feeling angry, this would just make them even angrier because they perceive you as someone who is hostile right from the beginning, even before you have said a word. If you want to be successful, you are going to need to hone your skills in both of these areas.

When communicating with an angry individual (or several), here is what you need to do:

> •**Think, hold and then speak** – To communicate effectively with angry people, you need to learn not to say the first thing that pops into your mind. Effective communicators, in general, are ones who think before they speak because they know that if they don't, they run the risk of saying the wrong thing or causing misunderstanding. It helps if you were to

hold off on responding immediately when dealing with an angry individual. Quickly run through what you were about to say and make sure it is okay and then only speak. Do not give in to the urge to respond with the first thing that pops into your head. It is completely okay to pause for a moment, take a beat to really think about what you're going to say, and then speak.

• **Using the right body language** – Even though you may not have any friendly feelings towards the person who is currently displaying their anger towards you, you would still need to make a conscious effort to keep your body language as welcoming as possible. Adopt an open, welcoming, and inviting body language because it is one of the most important factors you need to bear in mind when you're dealing with someone who is angry. Go back to the earlier scenario about what happens if when you're angry, you had to deal with someone who was equally hostile and making their annoyance blatant. What we are not saying outright can reveal more about how we really feel and body language is far more revealing than your words will ever be. Our bodies are capable of communicating without ever saying a word so watch your body language when you are having a conversation, especially with someone who is already emotional and angry. Maintain good eye contact, avoid crossing your arms in front of your chest, smile, don't put your hands in your pockets, and adopt a relaxed posture and hold your head up high with confidence.

• **Avoid mumbling too much** – You need to be able to speak clearly and project your voice when dealing with angry people. But not in a way that makes it appear as though you're shouting back at them. Just speak clearly enough to be heard over their raised tone of voice. Avoid being meek, soft and mumbling or muttering your words because they won't be able to hear what you're saying. If they can't hear you properly in their angry state, they could assume you're muttering something rude or offensive about them under your breath. This will only make them even angrier because they are already in a heightened emotional state as it is. Speak clearly and project, but maintain a respectful tone of voice.

• **Speak with patience** – You basically have to be the complete opposite of what the angry individual is. They are the emotional one, and you now need to be the calm and patient one. Speak in soothing tones and keep reminding yourself that this is not personal. They just happen to be very emotional right now, and they're not thinking straight. It is easy to get impatient with someone when they are unleashing their anger towards you with what seems like no regard for your feelings or emotions. Demonstrating your patience in a moment like this is a reflection on you as a person and how far you have come at managing your issues with anger. The fact that you can exude patience in a moment like this is something you should definitely be proud of because this is the ultimate demonstration of self-control.

The skills that you learned in this chapter will not only help you effectively manage the angry people that you have to deal with, but it will also give you some perspective into what other people have to put up with each time you fail to manage your anger. Use moments like this as a time for some internal reflection, to think about how this is what other people have to put up with whenever you're angry and treating them the same way. This can be one of those moments of clarity, where it dawns on you just how important it is to learn how to manage your anger because you don't want to continue treating other people this way. Use this as a great learning opportunity – because it is.

Chapter 10: Tricks and Tips – How to Handle Road Rage, Intimacy, and Other Specific Anger Issues

Having as many strategies, tips, and tricks for success can go a long way in helping you learn how to manage your anger much better, especially during specific moments like road rage, where it seems much harder to control yourself behind the wheel of your car. Or maybe you're in need of some advice about how to not let anger affect moments of intimacy.

Anger can be managed. It can be controlled, and it doesn't have to be a destructive force in your life. You have it within you to make these positive changes in your life for the better. With the additional tricks and tips that you will read about in this chapter, anger management is even easier than ever.

General Tips to Better Manage Your Anger

- **Have your own space** – Whether you're living alone or with someone, it helps to have a little space of your own at the end of the day where you can just spend a couple of minutes alone unwinding. Maybe create a little comfort zone of your own at home that helps promote feelings of calm and a sense of contentment. Turn a corner of your favorite room in your home into a special area where you can find your Zen and calm. Make this a space that you look forward to coming home to every day. This room should be free from distraction, makes you feel comfortable, and most importantly, it has to be somewhere that you want to be. Remove anything that can be a distraction, disconnect your phone, and shut yourself off from the world for just a few minutes each day where you can come and find and connect with yourself once more. It is a great way to center yourself and unwind after what may have been a long, tiring, and hectic day.

• **Exercise, make it a habit** – It cannot be stressed enough just how beneficial exercise can be for you. If you're not already working out regularly, start doing it. It is an excellent stress relief outlet, and you will feel better about yourself in a way you haven't before. It elevates your mood, keeps you fit and healthy, and more importantly, it is a way for you to let go of the pent-up emotions you've been carrying around all day. Just 30 minutes a day is all you need. Run it out. Kickbox it out. Dance it out. Do yoga if it helps you to relax. Exercise is one of the best remedies you can get your hands on when it comes to learning how to manage your anger, and if you're not already doing it, start now!

• **Start the day the right way** – Establishing a morning routine is one way to approach this. Having a great morning routine that leaves you charged up and energized is a great way to start every day on a positive, motivated note. If you've been waking up in a bad mood for far too long now, only thinking about the stress and everything you need to deal with for the day, it's time to change that. Why should you start developing a better morning routine for yourself? Because a morning routine or habit will help you focus your mind at the start of every day. It is a habit that successful people abide by, which would explain how they manage to stay optimistic, even in the face of great challenge. Incorporate a morning routine into your lifestyle that is going to help you clear your mind, stay focused, stay optimistic, and mentally prepare you for the rest of the day ahead.

• **Choose an activity a day which inspires you** – When was the last time you did something that inspired you to make a change for the better? That reawakened that motivation within you to want to do something to improve your life? If you can't even remember the last time you felt that way, you've been angry for far too long. What you need to do right now is start choosing activities which are going to inspire you. Doing this daily would be great, but if you can't manage that, several times a week would work too. Watch a Ted Talk, listen to inspirational podcasts, read biographies of successful people, or any inspirational books you can get your hands on. You'll find there are plenty of opportunities for you to do this during the day. For example, while you're on your lunch break, commuting to work, while you get ready in the morning or before going to bed at night. You could even do it while you take your short coffee breaks at work. There are plenty of opportunities all around you just waiting to be seized. All you need to do is start noticing them. And it only takes a few minutes to listen to something inspirational every day to keep you motivated doing what you love.

Having a morning routine or habit will help you focus your mind at the start of every day. Many notably successful people like Tony Robbins have been known to incorporate a morning routine into their lifestyle to help them clear their minds, stay focused, and mentally prepare for anything they need to do that day.

Tips to Help You Deal with Road Rage

Road rage is one of the most common reasons for getting angry while we're driving on the road. If this rings all too true to you, don't worry. Here are some effective strategies that you could use to help you stay much calmer on the road.

- **Avoid rushing** – Managing your time and being more organized can go a long way towards making a difference. Road rage is often triggered when you're in a hurry to get somewhere, and everything on the road seems to be delaying you. You get stressed, worked up, and increasingly frustrated as you realize you're closer to missing your appointment or running late to where you need to be. If you know there is somewhere you need to be, leave earlier than you initially planned to give yourself plenty of time to get there and minimize the reasons for the delay. For example, if you planned to leave by 10:00 am, adjust your schedule so that you leave at 9:30 am instead or earlier if you'd like. When you're not rushing, anxious, and pressed for time, it minimizes the aggravation that you feel when you are behind the wheel.

- **Relax in your car** – Are you tense each time you get behind the wheel? The next time you hop into your car, be mindful about how you're feeling. Do your shoulders feel tense? Are you gripping the wheel far too hard because you're feeling stressed? Taking some measures to relax before you even begin your drive can put you in a much calmer state. Maybe play your favorite relaxing tunes, or take a couple of deep, measured breaths as you adjust and get comfortable in the car. Smile and say today is going to be a great day as you buckle in. Relaxing or even playing a podcast that puts you in good spirits is a great way to set the tone for a good drive ahead.

• **Be considerate** – Being polite and courteous is not just an anger management method that is reserved only for when people are in front of you. This concept can even be applied when you're driving on the road. The road is a space for everyone; we all need to share. Nobody is entitled to anything. We all need to make an effort to be respectful of others on the road. Be polite and courteous even when you're driving. Give way to others instead of rushing to block them off and stop them from cutting in front of you. It never hurts to be politer. If other drivers are not, you don't have to be like them. Put yourself in the other driver's shoes. Maybe they are in a hurry to get somewhere for reasons of their own. If you were in a hurry, wouldn't you appreciate it each time someone gave you way without getting angry with you? Kindness can begin with you.

• **Avoid driving if you're in a bad mood** – There will be moments where you already leave your home in a bad mood because something happened. Beginning a drive in a bad mood is only going to aggravate your road rage tendencies. Instead, you should avoid driving altogether if you know that you're not exactly feeling your best. Maybe take an Uber that day and let someone else do the driving so you can make an effort to calm down in the back seat and put yourself in a better mood. Doesn't that sound like a better option? And it keeps your road rage tendencies at bay.

Keeping Anger Out of Your Relationships – Tips to Rebuild that Spark and Reconnect on an Intimate Level Again

Anger can put a great deal of strain on a relationship. It is not easy being around someone who frequently loses their temper, and even though they may apologize later for it, the emotional damage has already been done with the words that have been said. The actions that you do in anger, just like your words, can never be undone. This is what your partner is going through each time you're unable to manage your anger appropriately. Just because they love you, it doesn't make it any easier to put up with this part of your personality.

Which is why the best thing you can do for your relationship is to learn how to manage that anger. To bring the love, spark, and intimacy back into the relationship. To breathe life into it once more. The following tips will help you with this part of the process:

- **Talk to your partner** – This is the first step in the process. Talk to your partner, sit down, and have a real heart-to-heart with them. Let them know that you realize there is a problem and that you're doing everything you can to manage your anger better. Let them know how much you appreciate their love and support as you work on becoming better. Emphasize how appreciative you are for everything that they have done for you and that you're sincerely sorry for everything they have to put up with whenever you lose your temper. Having a deep, meaningful conversation will let your partner know what's happening and ensure that the two of you are on the same page. This makes it easier to lean on your partner for support in the moments that you need them.

- **Start spending time as a couple again** – It's easy to get caught up with your own schedules. There always never seems to be enough time to get everything done in a day. However, you need to *make* the time if you want to fix your relationship – do things that are fun, and have fun together, enjoying each other's company, especially if you've got a lot of work to do in rebuilding a relationship that has been damaged by anger. When you're having fun together and enjoying activities that bring you closer to each other, it helps to strengthen the bond that you have. It may even remind the two of you about what you loved most about each other in the first place (something which can easily be forgotten when too much anger has been thrown into the mix). For it to work effectively, pick activities that both of you enjoy doing together as a couple, not just an activity that one person is going to enjoy. Both of you need to equally have fun because that is how you bond and you're going to need to do a lot of bonding and healing to recover from the strain that anger has caused.

• **Keep reminding your partner how much you love and appreciate them** – It is easy for your partner to feel taken for granted if all they're getting is bursts of anger and temper tantrums from you. It can be easy to feel unloved when someone is always snapping at you. It's easy to question why you're in this relationship and putting up with all your partner's temper tantrums. These are all the perspectives you need to consider regarding what your partner may be going through each time you lose your temper and let anger take control, damaging the relationship. Which is why now, as part of your anger management exercise, you need to make it a point to constantly remind your partner how much you love and appreciate them at every opportunity you get.

Thoughts to Free Yourself from Anger

When we feel angry, we tend to forget that we always have a choice. Anger binds us into this narrow, tunnel vision way of thinking and looking at the world, which is why it is often so hard to overcome anger when it hits. To free yourself from anger and learn how to manage it better, you need to realize that:

• **Anger and people do not have power over you** – Nobody has power over you, not even your emotions. Nobody has the power to make you angry unless you *allow* them to make you angry. Your emotion does not have the power to get the best of you unless you *allow* it to. All the power sits with you, and when you realize that, you'll see how much easier it becomes to manage your anger, and the next time you find yourself in a situation which could potentially trigger your anger again, tell yourself, *Nope, I will not allow this to have the power to make me angry and walk away.*

• **What goes around comes around** – What you put out there in the world comes back to you. It may sound like just another clichéd saying, but it has truth to it. If you go about constantly angry, bitter, and upset all the time, ready to bite the head off the next person who annoys you, that is all you are going to see mirrored back at you. People won't be nice. People won't be kind. People won't be understanding. People appear grumpy, annoyed, and angry around you too. Why? Because this is what you're putting out there in the world. Try the opposite this time and put a little love and happiness out there instead, and see what gets reflected back at you.

• **People are not your enemies** – Nobody is going out of their way to make you angry on purpose. Nobody wants to go around purposely provoking others to anger. Sometimes, situations and circumstances just can't be helped, despite your best efforts. The sooner you realize that people are not your enemy, that they're not purposely setting out with the intention to raise your anger, the better it will be for you when it comes to keeping your anger under control. Learn to see people, even complete strangers, as your allies and friends. You never know where new connections could lead, what new opportunities could form from the relationships that you make.

Conclusion

Thank you for making it through to the end of this book. It should have been informative and provided you with all of the tools you need to achieve your goals, whatever they may be.

As you've seen, anger, when misdirected, can often result in great unhappiness for both you and the people around you. Poorly managed anger can be a source of great pain, but now you know that it doesn't have to be this way. Not in the least.

You have the power within you to learn how to channel your anger, control it, and manage it in far more positive ways, which will lead to more desirable, happier outcomes. When channeled correctly, your anger can be a source of great good which pushes you to accomplish your goals.

It is also important to remember to take the time to stop and appreciate just how far you have come with your efforts to manage your anger. Picking up this book and working with the strategies in it is already a major step in the right direction, and you should be proud that you're making the change to become a better, healthier version of yourself. You and the people around you will certainly appreciate how hard you're working towards keeping your anger under control.

With the strategies you are now equipped with, you will be well on your way to better anger management as long as you persevere and persist even in the challenging moments. One great tip to know for sure that things are changing for the better: you'll know you've made momentous strides when all the things that used to set off your anger before no longer bother you as much.

The journey to gaining control over your anger will be a journey that keeps on going, something that is always a work in progress. However, each day, you get better and each day is a new opportunity for you to grow stronger and gain an even firmer grasp on the emotion that once left you out of control. Take each day in stride as there is always something new to be learned, and most importantly, enjoy the journey because you're becoming a better version of yourself each day.

Finally, if you found this book useful in any way, a review on Amazon is always appreciated!

Check out more books by Steven Turner

EMPATH
Your Guide to Understanding Empaths and
Their Emotional Abilities to Feel Empathy,
Including Tips for Highly Sensitive People, Dealing
with Energy Vampires, and Being a Psychic Empath
Steven Turner

DARK PSYCHOLOGY
What Machiavellian People of Power Know about Persuasion, Mind Control, Manipulation, Negotiation, Deception, Human Behavior, and Psychological Warfare that You Don't
Steven Turner

DIALECTICAL
BEHAVIOR THERAPY
THE ULTIMATE GUIDE TO USING DBT FOR BORDERLINE PERSONALITY DISORDER, DIFFICULT EMOTIONS AND MOOD SWINGS, INCLUDING TECHNIQUES SUCH AS MINDFULNESS AND EMOTION REGULATION
STEVEN TURNER

www.ingramcontent.com/pod-product-compliance
Lightning Source LLC
Chambersburg PA
CBHW031251250726
48655CB00005B/2170